BEST FRIENDS
FOREVER
a couples guide

MICHAEL LEVIN

June 21, 2002

Dear Edward,
I hope this book helps you
to find the true love
of your life.

Warmest Regards,
Michael

For information address:
Best Friends Forever Press
4350 East Camelback Road
Suite F-100
Phoenix, Arizona 85018

LCCN pending

Library of Congress Cataloging-in-Publication Data

> Levin, Michael D.
> Best Friends Forever — A Couples Guide
> First paperback edition

ISBN: 0-9720777-0-7

Names and identifying characteristics of people in the book have been changed to protect the privacy of the individuals.

Cover and book design by Michele O'Hagan, 1106 Design, LLC, Phoenix, Arizona; (602) 866-3226; *www.1106design.com*

Cover sculpture, *Best Friends Forever* by Axel Soldwedel, Eisenart Innovations, Sedona, Arizona; *mail@eisenart.com*

Cover photo by Dave Tevis, Tevis Photographic, Tempe, Arizona; (480) 966-1230.

ACKNOWLEDGMENTS

I want to thank my father, Samuel B. Levin, for allowing me the opportunity to identify with a man who was truly the best friend to two women during his lifetime. I thank my mother, Lillian Sara Ziff Levin, for being my best friend and accepting and loving me so unconditionally, and for teaching me how to be a woman's best friend so early in my life. I want to thank my darling wife, Susan, for allowing me to share her very precious life and who inspires me daily with her insight, intelligence and devotion. She continues to allow me to be her best friend and for that I am forever indebted to her.

I thank my children — Dan, Marc, Jay, Tara, Ari and Adam. I thank Dan for teaching me that by simply persevering, we win. I thank Marc for his insight and unwavering love and devotion. I thank Jay for his clarity, genuine brilliance and for allowing me to share his mom with him. I thank Tara for paying me the greatest compliment I've ever received and for allowing me to be her friend. I thank Ari for lighting up my life every moment I think about him. And I thank Adam for the opportunity he may someday give me to earn his love and respect again.

I thank Howard and Noreen Wernick for their friendship, loyalty and love. I thank Noreen for the magnificent example she sets for all of us as a devoted and loving wife, mother and teacher, and for making us feel loved as though we were her immediate family. I want to thank Howard for setting the standard that every man, woman and child should strive to achieve; a standard of integrity, discipline, devotion to God, family and friends.

I want to extend my most sincere and heartfelt thanks to Barbara Balletto and Kate von Seeburg who edited this book. I want to thank Michele O'Hagan of 1106 Design in Phoenix for her book cover and interior design. I want to thank artist Axel Soldwedel for the *Best Friends Forever* sculpture and for his permission to use it on the cover of this book. And I want to thank every couple who trusted me enough to impact their minds, hearts and lives while I tried to guide them through the maze and pain of dissolving their marriage.

DEDICATION

This book is dedicated
to my wife
and the love of my life
Susan Hilary Grant.
Nobody does it better.

CONTENTS

FOREWORD

TO THOSE SEEKING LOVE

*S*ince June 1991 I have participated in the mediation of over 2,000 dissolutions of marriage. When each of those couples initially came into my office, they hoped that I could help them stop fighting long enough to reach agreement on custody of children, visitation rights, and division of all that stuff they accumulated during their marriage.

You know, they're not too different from you or me.

When they first met and fell in love with their future spouse, the only thing each of them wanted was to be held, loved, encouraged, told they are worthy, smiled at, flirted with, and made love to. They all had hope: hope that this person to whom they were so attracted would be their best friend for the rest of their life.

When couples come into my office, I generally ask each of them the same question: "What caused your marriage to fail?" These are the answers I hear:

"He yells at me and puts me down." "He doesn't care how I feel." "He only wants to be with his friends." "He's selfish." "All he does is work and he never spends time with me or the kids." "He never listens to what I think." "He embarrasses me when we're with our friends." "He never helps me around the house." "He lies to me." "He drinks and abuses drugs." "He doesn't appreciate anything I do for him." "He cares more about his family than me." "I had an affair."

"She doesn't trust me." "She's always yelling at me." "She doesn't appreciate how hard I work." "She doesn't understand how much pressure I'm under." "She spends too much money." "She's always complaining." "She is always criticizing me." "She only cares about herself." "She thinks she's always right." "She drinks and abuses drugs." "She doesn't like my family." "She's always trying to change me." "She had an affair, but so did I."

On occasion, while listening to them tell me the reasons why they couldn't live with their respective spouse, I find myself conjuring up the image of them standing at the altar, in front of all of their loving friends and family to share that wonderfully incredible moment, while they declare their everlasting love and devotion to all who are listening. And I wonder — how could this have happened? What went wrong? They each wanted and needed to love and be loved, to be accepted, to be made to feel worthy, and to have someone they could trust as their mate.

I've concluded that — in most cases — relationships fail for the following reasons:

1. They chose the wrong partner.
2. They didn't take time to thoroughly exchange personal and family backgrounds so that they understood their partner.
3. They broke both implied and verbal promises to each other.
4. They said or did things that caused their partner to feel abandoned.
5. They had not been taught how to be their partner's best friend.

Initially, almost every woman will try to do everything possible to make her man feel loved. She'll be as sexy as she can be; she'll make love to him anytime he wants; she'll cook his favorite meals; she'll be sympathetic of how tired he is when he comes home from work; and she'll take care of most of their responsibilities around the home. But as time passes, if she feels abandoned by him and is unable to help him to understand what she is feeling, she begins to build a barrier to protect her both from the emotional and sometimes physical pain he inflicts upon her and from the perception that he doesn't love her. That barrier continues to grow each time he breaks promises or causes her to feel abandoned. She no longer responds to his needs. He feels frustrated by not understanding why she is not doing the same things for him. He is frustrated by the fact that she doesn't trust him and wants him to be different.

Almost every man too, will initially try to do everything to make his partner feel loved. He'll work hard at his job. He'll bring her flowers and write little love notes. He'll take her out for dinner when she hasn't had time to prepare it. But as time passes — if she is demanding and demeaning rather than appreciative and supportive, if she insists on having it her way and doesn't compromise easily, and if she makes him feel that she's abandoned him (for example, by siding with her family against him) — he, too, builds a barrier that may be impossible to penetrate.

Women inherently seem to know how to be a man's best friend — but when women find themselves in a relationship with a man who is not being *their* best friend, they likely will choose not to be *his* best friend, either.

Too many men, I have found, simply do not know *how* to be a woman's best friend. Some men have not had the benefit of learning this art by being their mom's best friend; others may not have had a father with whom they could identify who was their mom's best friend. Although these men are well meaning and initially want to love their partner in all the right ways, it doesn't come naturally to them — through no fault of their own.

Many a woman doesn't recognize this lack of knowledge on the part of her chosen man — she doesn't realize that he needs to be taught and that *she* is the one who needs to do the teaching.

When barriers are built, the peaceful, warm, sensitive, intuitive interaction that is necessary for a healthy, loving relationship cannot flow back and forth from one partner to the other. Both withdraw and hide behind their own barrier. The struggle of survival becomes increasingly more difficult. Neither feels loved. Both are defensive and feel that they have to carry the burden of the struggle of life themselves. They each try to reach out to the other once in a while, but rarely are both ready to drop their own defenses at exactly the same time. Finally, the frustration of each being shut out of each other's life is too great and the relationship fails.

While listening to couples tell me why their marriage failed, a feeling of sadness comes over me. We struggle to improve ourselves, succeed at our jobs, pay our bills, remain emotionally well balanced, and raise our children to become happy, productive human beings. Every day we hope that we or someone we love doesn't become ill. Much of the time, we feel as if we're just barely clinging to our sanity. Doesn't it seem reasonable that when we find that one person to whom we are willing to commit to loving for our entire lifetime, that at least we shouldn't have to struggle to maintain a healthy, loving relationship with that person?

Well, it seems reasonable to me.

Best Friends Forever: A Couples Guide is written to help those of us seeking love to find and maintain a loving relationship forever. If you're already *in* a relationship, it is the guide you and your partner should try to follow every day of your lives together. If you do, neither of you will ever have a need to build a barrier that separates one from the other. You'll "make love" from the time you get up in the morning until the time you fall asleep — by doing things for each other that make your lives more comfortable. You'll be encouraging positive feelings of self worth in each other. You will trust each other implicitly. Your partner will know that you are on their side all of the time, and you'll know they're on yours.

You'll love how good that feels.

You may even want to share this feeling with *your* best friends.

I know I've found that feeling with *my* best friend (who also happens to be my wife). And I'd like to share it with you.

— Michael Levin

INTRODUCTION

THE EVOLUTION OF
A GREAT RELATIONSHIP

*T*hose of us who are blessed to have a great relationship with our partner know that this relationship evolves through several stages. (The duration of each stage is irrelevant — a shorter first stage, for example, does not signify that your relationship is less wonderful than a couple whose first stage lasts for a few years.)

Stage 1: You and your partner first meet and the electricity between the two of you is at such a high pitch that you can barely keep your hands off of each other. Depending upon many variables, this stage can last from a few months to a few years.

Stage 2: You and your partner are still highly sexually attracted to one another, but it's not as "hot" an attraction as while you were passing through Stage 1. The portion of the slightly reduced sexually "hot" stage begins to be replaced with a peacefulness and comfort that comes from just being in each other's presence. Once again, this stage may last from another few years to perhaps as many as 10 years or more.

Stage 3: You and your partner have passed through the lustful stage of your relationship. You still have a really good sexual relationship. It's fun. It's sensual. You both still consciously want to please each other. Kissing, although perhaps not as passionate as it may have once been, still feels as warm and sensual as the first time you kissed each other. You still "play" with each other in terms of the sexual context of some of your remarks, but having sex and being "in lust" has been replaced with a comfort level of being with your partner that has never been surpassed by any other relationship you've ever experienced. You trust your partner so explicitly not to hurt you that you're totally peaceful in their presence. You know from the consistency of how your partner acts and reacts to being with you that there isn't anything you can say that would elicit a shocking response. You can play with each other comfortably and you can argue with each other peacefully. You trust that your partner will never touch one of your "insecure" spots — even if they're angry. During this stage you've probably never experienced a happier period of time during your life. You realize how blessed you are to be able to share your life with your best friend and you cherish every day because of it. Regardless of how difficult life seems to be, you know that while being at home — with your best friend — you're safe and loved. Stage 3 in the evolution of a great relationship is by far the longest stage.

Stage 4: You and your partner are approaching 70 years of age. You both know that the years ahead, in terms of your health, may not be easy. You both begin to feel afraid of the prospect of losing the "love of this lifetime." You carry on each day suppressing those feelings of fear. You hold your love a little closer. You hold on a little longer. Once in a while when the feeling surfaces you try not to cry — even inside — at the fear you're beginning to feel about your best friend becoming ill. Your love is so strong it's difficult to imagine any other two people loving each other so much. She still makes you tingle by just the way she looks at you. He makes you smile a little while just watching him. Sex is probably as great as ever.

Stage 5: I can hardly even write about acknowledging this stage. You're approaching 90 to 95 years now. You've been pretty darn healthy throughout your love affair because of the peacefulness you've felt while spending your life with your best friend. This peacefulness and feeling of being so loved has helped you maintain emotional stability, which in turn has helped you to be physically healthy. But, alas — the time for you to part during this lifetime is coming near. Intellectually you know that you've been blessed. Emotionally, you're afraid to be alone. And then, one of you passes over. Now listen carefully to me, please. Your best friend is *still with you*. Oh, certainly they're not *physically* present, but close your eyes and feel their presence. Ask them a question. They will answer you. Your angel in life is still your angel. Feel them. Speak with them. Share with them and soon you will be together again. Your souls will meet again. Your love will share that love once again. And you will continue to be blessed with peacefulness for eternity.

And what is that key element necessary to have this wonderfully loving relationship?

Honesty. Not just the kind of honesty I speak about when, in *A Man's Guide To Being A Woman's Best Friend* (Appendix A), I say "Tell the truth about everything, even the smallest detail." It is a much deeper level of honesty than that.

It's that level of honesty that we "sometimes" share, but should share more often, if only with ourselves. It's that level of honesty that we suppress quickly if we're embarrassed. It's such a high level of honesty that we expose most elements of ourselves to that person with whom we are falling in love. Now that's a scary thought. Am I saying that we have to allow that potentially life-long best friend — who is beginning to believe that we are so wonderful — to learn the real truth about us? Yes, that's exactly what I'm saying. You must understand, though, that nearly all of us have done — and maybe currently are doing — things of which we are ashamed. I'm not saying, however, that you have to sit down with your new love and start telling them your deepest, darkest, most embarrassing shameful secrets. I am saying, though, that to create a beautifully peaceful partnership with another human being you must be, from the very first day you meet until the last day you're with them, absolutely truthful about your entire being and every element of your life. You have to be open to hearing and accepting the truth — especially if it's your best friend telling you the truth — no matter how much that truth hurts. And, most importantly, you have to begin telling the truth to yourself.

You have to allow your best friend to feel safe sharing their feelings with you. This means you can't be defensive. And your best friend must be a good enough friend to not only allow *you* to do the same, but also they must love you enough to be gentle — not hurtful — when telling you their perception. You have to remember that their perception is just that: *their perception*. You may not fully agree with it, but it *is* their perception. If you don't accept it, try to understand it. Attempt to compromise your perception with their perception. If you do so, you will be blessed with a very special love.

But wait — there's still more. When it comes to your best friend you must never do or say anything that makes you less worthy of their love. From the moment you give them the impression that you want to be loved by them, you have to commit to never doing anything of which you would be ashamed or of which you would tend to hide or not be honest about. If you fail in this, you have to dig down deep and — whether you like it or not — tell your partner the truth. For each of us to achieve true peacefulness within our relationships, we must trust that our partner is always telling us the truth.

Further, if you are a man, you must commit to doing everything contained in Appendix A in the back of this book. If you are a woman, you must commit to doing everything contained in Appendix B. There are no exceptions. You also have to allow your partner to see your deepest, darkest fears; to hear your dreams and to see your weaknesses. You have to share the story of your lifetime with your partner so that they are aware of how you've previously been hurt by those you've loved. Your partner, of course, must do the same with you. No matter what occurs, the two of you may never — and I mean *never* — use the knowledge of that previous hurt to hurt the other partner again. It doesn't matter how angry you may be. You can't ever touch on a spot that you know will be painful to your partner. If you do, you are breaching a trust that may never again be achieved. The words "I'm sorry" don't make a breach of trust disappear. And that trust, my dear readers, is what achieving the evolution of a great relationship is all about.

PART ONE

Who Is Mr./Ms. Right?

Chapter 1

IT'S MORE THAN
ANIMAL MAGNETISM

*W*e're not all lucky enough to have experienced it: that feeling you get when you meet someone new and it seems as though you've known them before. It's a feeling of peacefulness that makes you feel like smiling ever so slightly. Some have described it as feeling like they've come home; it's that comfortable. Yet you're sure that you have not met them before — in this lifetime, at least. It can happen anywhere. You can be standing on one side of the produce section in the market. He's on the other side. You look up for just a moment and there he is. You can be casually roaming through an open house one spring Sunday afternoon, when suddenly you see her. The feeling is remarkable. You never forget exactly how you felt at that moment. You're fortunate to experience it. Most of us who have experienced it refer to it as "love at first sight," but we know it's something more. It's a great feeling, no mistake about it, but it's far from enough to be able to say "this is the person I will be devoted to for the rest of my life."

Whether we feel as though we have fallen in love at first sight or we have fallen in love less suddenly, it's important to remain aware of our tendency to be vulnerable, because we all have a need to feel loved. We need to be loved so badly we're all susceptible to fooling ourselves into thinking "this is the one." Any woman wants to hear a man say, "you're beautiful," "you're funny," "you're so smart," "just being with you excites me." All men want to hear a woman say "you're so strong and soooo big, and I love being with you."

■ LOVE IS BLIND

When we meet someone new to whom we're attracted, we tend to remain oblivious to their less desirable personality traits. We begin the relationship by pretending those negative traits simply don't exist. We don't mention them and we try not to think about them. The problem occurs when we suppress thoughts of those negative traits so completely that we only focus on our new partner's positive traits. We convince ourselves that those negative traits will magically disappear, perhaps because the passion of our love will dissolve them. Finally, we fool ourselves for so long, we find ourselves married to a person who — for a variety of reasons — we shouldn't have married.

So who is the right person? What are the positive personality traits on which we should focus and the negative ones of which we should be wary? Throughout this first part of *Best Friends Forever, A Couples Guide*, we'll examine the dynamics of the failed relationships of couples for whom I've mediated a dissolution of marriage. We'll examine what positive personality traits each participant in the relationship exhibited — as well as those that may have been a factor in causing the marriage to fail. But you'll also see how couples can *learn* from their past mistakes: from time to time I'll also relate the story of how a victim of a failed relationship has moved on to a new, successful relationship. (It's interesting to see how their new partner's personality traits stack up against those of their former partner.)

Make no mistake: I'm not saying you'll be able to find a partner who is perfect. However, after reading this book, you *should* expect to have a heightened awareness concerning your partner's characteristics and their importance in a relationship. It is my hope that you will be aware of, appreciate, and reinforce positive characteristics — but that you won't ignore the existence of negative characteristics or pretend that they don't exist so you can temporarily continue to feel loved.

By being able to see which characteristics are negative and which are positive, you should be better able to understand what personality traits "Mr. or Ms. Right" should or shouldn't possess. Armed with this new-found greater awareness, you should be able to choose your partner more carefully and have a better chance to build a loving, fulfilling, long-term relationship — one in which you are best friends forever.

■ BE YOURSELF (AND LET YOUR PARTNER DO THE SAME)

If you wish there were things about your new love that were different, there's one basic thing you need to remember: *People generally don't change* (significantly). We all want to believe that if we love someone enough and if we give enough of ourselves to them, they will become different in the ways we wish they were different. In the majority of the cases, it is just not going to happen. True, people may try to change — and for short periods of time they may succeed. But eventually, when they are not able to become all that you want them to be, you'll both resent being with one another. We need to be willing to accept our partners the way they are — or let them go.

You should always feel comfortable simply being yourself. You shouldn't feel that you have to pretend to be someone you're not in order to be accepted. For example, if you try to be open and honest about your feelings, but when you do your new love responds by saying "How can you say something like that...you must be crazy," you will feel that you can't express your true feelings without being criticized. Are you going to be open and honest the next time? Probably not. You undoubtedly will begin to avoid sharing your feelings — or you'll tend to say things that you think will get a positive response from your partner.

■ A NEED FOR APPROVAL

Let's say that one evening you're getting ready to go out. You choose clothes in which you think you'll look best. You finish getting dressed. Your partner takes one look and says, "Don't you have anything else to wear?" After this happens even a couple of times, you'll begin to question your own judgement, and will look for their approval before making a decision of which clothes to wear. That need for approval (or fear of disapproval) may carry over to other aspects of your relationship, and it will be difficult for you to feel comfortable when you're with your partner.

If you feel like you need your partner's full approval to feel accepted, you'll find it difficult to be relaxed just being yourself. You may feel like you're walking on eggshells when you're in their presence.

This is the feeling we have when we're feeling controlled. If you remain in a relationship in which you are feeling controlled, you'll eventually feel resentful. You'll be angry at yourself for needing to be loved and accepted so badly that you allow yourself to be with a person who wants you to act or be different and tries to change you. You may find it's better to be your own best friend and remain alone, than to be with someone who doesn't like you the way you are most naturally and tries to change you.

If you remain in a controlling relationship, you will project that anger you feel for yourself at your partner. You will say things like "nothing I do is right," or "it's impossible to please you." You will blame your inability to feel comfortable in their presence on them, when in truth you're angry at yourself. You'll feel angry because you had fair warning. Your partner probably implied early in the relationship that their love was conditional. They told you by their actions or words that there were things about you they wanted to be different. Don't blame them because you agreed to accept their controlling nature.

■ READ THE WARNING SIGNS: A CASE IN POINT

Karen (the true name of mediation participants throughout this book have been changed to protect their privacy), who was married to Bernie, had not graduated from college. Bernie, on the other hand, had graduated college and graduate school. I mediated their dissolution of marriage in June 1993.

Karen liked to watch her soaps. Bernie ridiculed soap opera programs as appealing to stupid, uneducated people who didn't realize that reading was the way to improve their minds. One Saturday evening when Bernie and Karen were at a restaurant with another married couple, Karen asked her female friend whether she had watched the Thursday segment of _____.

Before her friend even had a chance to answer, Bernie piped up, "How can you watch those stupid programs? They're only for uneducated idiots." Then he casually continued his conversation with his male friend. Karen, of course, was humiliated. She never verbally responded to Bernie's demeaning remark, but she told us that she felt as though he had physically punched her in the stomach.

Bernie believed that because Karen wasn't as well read or as educated as he was, anything she thought was interesting — including her soap operas — was meant for someone who didn't need to be intellectually stimulated. He didn't respect Karen's intellectual ability, so he didn't speak to her or treat her as his equal.

When Bernie made that comment to Karen during their dinner, he embarrassed her terribly. Unfortunately for both of them, this wasn't the first time Bernie had embarrassed Karen in front of their friends. It was just another time that Bernie hurt Karen, which caused her to shut down emotionally in order to protect herself from him.

From time to time Karen tried to explain to Bernie how she felt. One particular weekday evening, Karen related, she had decided to try to help Bernie understand how he was making her feel. She made a special dinner of all of Bernie's favorite foods; she showered after she got home from work, washed her hair, and styled it the way Bernie liked to see her wear it. She even put on a blouse that fell slightly off her shoulders because Bernie often made positive comments when he saw other women dressed in a similar fashion.

Bernie came home, and the first words out of his mouth were, "Boy, am I tired. My day was lousy. The traffic was heavy and there was a terrible accident. What's for dinner?" Not only didn't he say anything about how much attention Karen had paid to making herself look beautiful for him, he never kissed her, or even said "Hi, how was your day?" He certainly didn't notice Karen had made a special effort to make his favorite things for dinner. When he and Karen sat down for dinner, Bernie began to talk about how a particular client of his liked him so much. Finally, when Karen saw an opening, she said "Bernie, I want to tell you how I felt when you inferred that I was stupid when we were out with Jay and Tara." Bernie responded, "Can't we just enjoy this dinner? Or do you have to make my day even more miserable than it already has been?" Bernie didn't even have the sensitivity to look at Karen when she was asking him to listen to her.

Karen was afraid to bring the subject up again that evening because she felt certain it would result in a fight. Later that evening, Bernie became angry when Karen didn't want to make love.

What can we learn from this one incident from Bernie and Karen's relationship? We can learn that if you choose to be with someone who is controlling and who feels intellectually superior to you, you may be committing to a person who will say things to you that will cause you to feel unworthy. They may have a tendency to patronize you and make demeaning remarks to you, both privately and in public.

But here's the heart of the matter: Karen confided that Bernie treated her the same way while they were dating, too. She said that he made her feel as though she had nothing interesting to say, but she said she felt good being with someone like Bernie who was so confident, well educated, and well read that she overlooked his demeaning remarks and criticism. She interpreted his derogatory comments as being his way of trying to help her to improve herself — after all, Bernie himself had said, "If I can't tell you things like that, who will?" The problem, of course, was that Bernie undermined Karen's feelings of self worth, and they continued to diminish while she remained married to him.

Remarkably, Bernie was never able to understand why Karen wanted to dissolve their marriage. He made a great living. They lived in a beautiful home and he purchased a new car for her every other year. What Bernie should have realized is that if he wanted Karen to be his best friend, he should have understood that, to her, listening was a critical aspect of "foreplay." He should have understood that when he was critical of her, he not only was being controlling but also he caused her to feel unworthy. He should have also understood that it was necessary for him to make good eye contact with Karen, and give her his undivided attention when she wanted to express her pain.

Each time Bernie said things that caused Karen to feel unworthy, she shut down a little more in order to protect herself from being hurt. Verbal abuse was as devastating to her as physical abuse would have been. Karen went through the motions of being with Bernie for years, but he hurt her, he was not her friend, and she couldn't trust him.

■ A NEW START WITH NEW KNOWLEDGE

Interestingly, Karen called me about a year after her dissolution was final and said she had been accepted into the nursing program at a local community college, and — perhaps ironically — was using her half of Bernie's 401K plan to pay for her education. She said that there was a new man in her life who was well educated like Bernie, but who listened to her perspective — even if he didn't always agree with it. She felt good being with him, and she was feeling good about herself. Karen still liked to watch her soaps — but this time her new love liked to keep up with them, too. Karen helped him to do that over dinner, which sometimes he made when she was late arriving home from school. Laughing, she told me, "I didn't know life could be so wonderful."

■ A MATTER OF PRIVACY — AND TRUST

We all need our privacy — it has nothing to do with trying to hide something. It's simply that we all need to retain our individuality, and maintaining our privacy is a big part of that. Privacy is strongly linked to trust — and without trust in a relationship, that relationship is destined for trouble.

Take Betsy and Andy. They had just celebrated their 18th wedding anniversary when they first called me. Well, actually *Andy* called me, but as I learned during that call, Betsy was listening in, too — although Andy wasn't aware of it at first. Andy said that he just couldn't stand it any longer. Betsy had been abusing alcohol for years, her chain smoking drove him nuts because she always smelled of smoke, and she wouldn't allow him to have any privacy. She was always checking up on him no matter what he was doing. Betsy quickly made me aware that Andy couldn't be trusted. She said, "He's just like my father. He would screw around as soon as he had the chance." She said that she couldn't help herself to feel secure, and nothing Andy said made any difference. She had to check up on him.

Betsy and Andy had four children, who were ages 16, 14, 11, and 3. Betsy had not worked outside the house during their marriage — although, as she said, "Who has time when you have four kids to raise?" Andy was employed by a large computer chip manufacturer as an engineer. He earned about $55,000 per year, including overtime, which usually was about 10 hours per week. Andy noted that they never had enough money and were deeply in debt because Betsy couldn't stop spending money on clothes for herself. Betsy couldn't understand why that was so important to Andy, because her parents gave her money to buy clothes for herself.

At the first mediation session, Andy wanted to begin talking — saying that he just couldn't hold it in any longer. He said that ever since they got married, Betsy didn't trust him. He admitted that it probably wasn't all her fault, because her father continually had affairs while he was married to Betsy's mother. Betsy's mother, Andy noted, was an alcoholic, too — like Betsy. Andy also complained that, from the very beginning of their relationship, Betsy would open his mail even though he asked her not to do it. She would call his work when he said he had to work overtime, just to see if he was there. She said she just needed to hear his voice because she was so in love with him, but Andy knew she was checking up on him. Andy continued by saying that Betsy would sort through everything in his wallet at least once each month. He felt as though he had absolutely no privacy.

When Andy would come home from work, Betsy would complain about how they never had enough money. She would compare Andy to her friends' husbands, who were able to afford a new car, take vacations twice each year, and weren't forced to have to take money from their parents. When Andy tried to explain that he was working as many hours as he could, she'd say that he would just have to find another way to make more money. Eventually, Andy admitted, he tried to work overtime just so he could stay away from Betsy longer.

A couple of times Betsy even said that she wished she had married Frank, whom she dated just before meeting Andy. Frank, she pointed out, at least had a secure job and made lots of money while working in his family's business.

Andy also said that Betsy always had to be right about everything. He complained that she just didn't know how it felt to be living with someone who never compromised. If Betsy and he were going out to dinner on the weekend, it had to be the restaurant *she* picked. If Betsy and he were going to buy a car, it had to be the car *she* had to have. He said that it was intolerable. He had no right to do anything he wanted to do. He couldn't even watch a basketball game on television without Betsy complaining that he never had time for her.

■ BETSY'S STORY

Betsy, on the other hand, said that it wasn't her fault: Andy just didn't know how it felt to be so neglected. She said all he did was work. When he came home he said he was so tired that all he could do was watch television. She was the one who raised the kids. She'd be damned if he was going to get joint custody like he wanted. Betsy said that she was stuck in the house all day and that her only pleasure was shopping. Of course she wanted to go out at night, after putting up with the kids all day. Yes, she knew Andy was tired, but she needed the break from being at home all day.

Andy swore that he hadn't had an affair. He said that there was one woman at work with whom he was friends, but that he never even kissed her — although he also said that he may as well have had an affair, because Betsy was sure he did. Betsy couldn't understand why the two had to work together so late and Andy explained the woman worked in his department and that was the way it was. Betsy commented, "Sure, that's what my father said, too."

Given Betsy's apparent obsession with her father's abandonment of her mother, Betsy may not be able to feel secure in any relationship without counseling. As a result of her insecurity, Betsy continually did things like open Andy's mail and look through his wallet — a big-time invasion of Andy's privacy. If Betsy needed to get something that she knew was in his wallet, she should have brought it to him so he could have retrieved it for her. It's a way she could have showed him that she respected his privacy. It was a way she could have helped him to feel comfortable in her presence.

Andy, for his part, then thought that going through Betsy's purse to find receipts for clothing purchases was acceptable behavior. Another invasion of privacy: A woman's purse is as personal as her diary. To both men and women, wallets and purses are places to keep highly personal things and information that they carry with them daily. It's the place both of them keep "their" money. It's the place where they each hide those few extra dollars they are saving for something important.

■ DON'T COMPARE

Betsy continually made Andy feel inadequate by comparing him to her friends' husbands. She didn't understand that until they reach about 21 years of age, male children are asked the following question dozens and dozens of times: "What are you going to be when you grow up?" — which really means "How are you going to earn enough money to support your family when you reach adulthood?" As they grow into their mid-teens, parents and teachers begin to convey the message that they must perform well in school if they're going to get a good job. And as they graduate high school and either attend college or venture out into the workplace, the pressure to find a way to earn a good living intensifies. Even if — as is the case in many of today's relationships — both partners work, most men still feel an age-old pressure to be the primary wage earner.

If Betsy wanted to be Andy's best friend, she should have remained aware of this pressure. There are too many times that we struggle financially just to break even. Most of the time we're not only struggling to break even, we're struggling to find a miracle in order to catch up. Betsy should have been conscious of times when Andy was feeling an extraordinary amount of pressure and not add to this pressure by spending too much money. She should have tried to make him understand that whatever financial problem he was facing was her problem, too.

To be perfectly honest, though, as hard as she may have tried to help him understand that fact, she wouldn't have been able to ease the pressure he was feeling. He's the man of the family. He feels that he's the one responsible for supporting his family. The more a woman comments on material things her friends have been able to buy, the more she wishes out loud, the more it makes "the man of the house" feel like he's not succeeding in meeting his responsibilities. It makes the struggle that much greater.

Betsy also compared Andy to her former boyfriend Frank. She accepted money from her parents on a regular basis in order to be able to buy more clothes for herself, and although Andy implied that he was doing his best to earn as much money as possible, Betsy said that his best wasn't good enough, he would just have to earn more money. Every time Betsy would hurt Andy in this way, he felt as though Betsy had betrayed him. Eventually, as he said to us when he called, he couldn't take it anymore.

■ THE PRICE OF NOT TRUSTING

For our purposes here, let's assume that Andy was a good man. He didn't abuse Betsy verbally or physically, he tried to be loving and giving, and was attentive until she apparently drove him away. We also know that he was a hard-working man who earned a pretty good living. For now, we're not going to look at what may be the "other side of the story" that Betsy or many other women could tell about their "Andy." We're just going to focus on Betsy and what effect her not trusting Andy had on their relationship.

Remember, Betsy was always checking up on Andy. When he said that he was working overtime, Betsy called his office to make sure he was there. She looked through his wallet. She listened in on his phone conversations: The phone call he made to us regarding mediation was not the first time she had done this. Through her manipulative actions, Betsy caused Andy to have a persistent feeling of being controlled. He felt resentful that Betsy didn't trust him. He began to have feelings of doubt about his own honesty. During one of our mediation sessions, he confessed: "I began to wonder if I was doing something which should *make* Betsy feel that way. Sure, I was working overtime hours with Linda, one of my co-workers, and we talked sometimes — as co-workers do. I liked her, but I never felt any emotional or physical feelings for her — until I began to feel rebellious because Betsy was showing me that she didn't think I could be trusted. Even then, I only thought about kissing Linda. I never did."

It's interesting. Andy said that he didn't have any feelings for Linda *until Betsy made him feel as though he couldn't be trusted.* I believe that only then did he seem to say to himself "What the heck, if she doesn't trust me, and there's nothing I can do to convince her that I should be trusted, I may as well become more friendly with another woman." I'm sure that Andy's thought process wasn't well defined. And I'm pretty sure that he didn't actually have the thought, "I may as well have an affair with Linda." The feeling of not being trusted made him feel rebellious. That feeling of rebelliousness led to his first physical feeling for Linda. So the question here is: by opening his mail, by listening in on his phone conversations, and by checking up on him, did Betsy push him into have feelings for another woman?

The answer may very well be YES.

Mr./Ms. Right is a person who trusts that you will always tell the truth. They're a person who doesn't check up on you and cause you to feel guilty when there's no reason for you to feel guilty. They're a person who doesn't cause you to have doubts about your own truthfulness.

■ A LITTLE APPRECIATION GOES A LONG WAY

Best friends love to do things for each other — and they don't expect anything in return. But just as important as the act of *doing* is the act of *receiving*. If you truly are a "best friend forever," you will be appreciative of anything your partner does for you: your eyes will sparkle ever so slightly, a small smile will cross your face, and you'll utter a heartfelt "Thank you, honey." That's showing appreciation — it's that simple.

From time to time, women and men for whom I've mediated dissolutions tell me that they are happily involved in a new love relationship. When this happens, it isn't unusual for me to ask what specifically is different about this relationship and the one with their former spouse. Such was the case when Katherine called to tell me that she was remarrying and asked me to attend her wedding.

One of Katherine's biggest complaints about her 22-year marriage to Robert was that it seemed impossible for her to please him. Not so with her new love, Karl. Katherine and Karl dated for over a year, and then decided to live together. He, too, had been married previously.

As an example of how different Karl is from Robert, Katherine related how one particular evening she arrived home at 5:30 and found she didn't have much of anything in the house for dinner. So she threw a couple of potatoes in the oven to bake, put some lettuce and tomatoes into a bowl and added a little dressing, and put some cottage cheese, still in the container, on the table. Karl came home, kissed Katherine hello, and cleaned up a little. When Karl walked into the kitchen, Katherine said, "I'm really sorry, honey...I didn't have time to prepare dinner. All I have is a baked potato with some cottage cheese, and salad." Karl's response? "That's great, honey — you know, that was exactly what I've been thinking about all day."

Of course it turns out — as Katherine tells it — that Karl *always* says that, whether Katherine spends an hour or more preparing dinner or only 10 minutes. Katherine considers herself to be responsible for preparing dinner each evening, even though she works outside the home in a fulltime job (as does Karl). But Katherine indicates that Karl prepares dinner for *her* at least a couple of times each week, and once in a while — although they don't have much extra money — Karl takes her out when she hasn't had time to prepare dinner. She says that one really interesting difference between Karl and Robert is that Karl understands how time-consuming — to say nothing of mind-consuming — the responsibility of preparing dinner can be. He realizes that Katherine wants dinner to be nutritional and well balanced; that she wants variety. He realizes that she wants it to be creative, to look and taste good, and to be prepared on time because she knows he is hungry when he gets home.

"Karl," says Katherine, "knows that taking me out to dinner when I haven't had time to prepare dinner is more of a gesture to show that he loves me than bringing me a dozen red roses."

Karl, unlike Robert, appreciates that Katherine is really carrying two full-time jobs: she teaches high school and is also primarily responsible for preparing dinner, taking care of the household responsibilities and taking care of him. He says thank you when she prepares dinner. He sometimes prepares her children's school lunches. He helps her clean the house. He cleans the bathroom sink and wipes the water spots off of the mirror. He picks his clothes up off of the floor. He replaces the empty roll of toilet paper. He removes the dishes from the dinner table after dinner. Karl, unlike Robert, shows Katherine by his actions that he is not oblivious to the amount of work with which she has to cope each day. Katherine doesn't feel angry or resentful like she did when she was with Robert, because Karl is cognizant of her work load.

In a nutshell, Karl seems to know a lot more about being a woman's best friend than Robert.

■ COMPROMISE AND ADMIT YOUR MISTAKES

Karl also loves to do things for Katherine — unlike Robert, who only expected Katherine to do things for him. Every morning, Karl brings Katherine coffee and gets back into bed to cuddle with her. He knows that she hates to empty the dishwasher or take out the garbage, so he does that for her. Katherine admits that they don't always agree on everything, but the one thing that makes being with Karl enjoyable for her is that he compromises easily. If she wants to go to the movies and he wants to stay home, he goes to the movies with her even though he may be a little tired. But it works both ways: at other times when Karl is tired, Katherine says she is happy to make having a quiet evening at home on a Friday or Saturday night seem just perfect to her.

There's one last thing that Katherine noted which is really worth sharing. When Karl does mess up (although frankly that's apparently not too often), he readily apologizes. But when Katherine screws up — which she says is much too often — Karl doesn't expect her to apologize. He hardly even mentions it at all, choosing rather to say something like, "It's no big deal, honey".

However, being considerate of one another — like Katherine and Karl — is not enough. We must be conscientious, too. We all have to bear some responsibility for providing a decent standard of living for ourselves. The days of the man being the only or primary wage earner are long gone. Two incomes are now a necessity just to provide the basics.

There are exceptions, of course. There are circumstances where one partner is lucky enough to earn sufficient income to provide the standard of living to which both partners aspire. But that situation shouldn't be taken for granted. Even if you are the fortunate recipient of a lovely home, a nice car, and being able to "shop till you drop," you must be conscientious about taking care of the details of running the business of life itself, so your partner can concentrate during normal working hours on their job.

And in a double-income home, the partner who is making the greater income must be aware that their job is not more important than their partner's. They mustn't attempt to dominate the relationship or make their partner feel less significant. Being condescending to your partner does not win points. If you're tuning in to your partner's mind, when you say or do something that is condescending, you can actually hear them say to themselves, "Jerk!" That's one attitude that doesn't make sense if you're trying to be your partner's best friend.

■ HOW THE PAST RELATES TO THE FUTURE

It's important in any "best friends forever" relationship to know as much as you can about your partner's past — their childhood, their schooling, their relationships with parents and siblings, and so forth — to understand how they came to be the person they are today. (*See Part Two: The Passkey to the Door of Your Past, page 61.*)

But equally important — before any lasting commitments are made — is that you understand how your partner's past patterns are likely to influence your life as a couple. Here's an example of how understanding a person's past actions — and reading a relationship right from the start, at the "dating stage" — can give you a glimpse into the future.

In late 1994 I mediated the dissolution of the marriage of a couple I'll refer to as Jonathan and Emily. When they were referred to me by a marriage counselor, Jonathan and Emily had been married 10 years. They had one six-year-old child. During those 10 years, Jonathan had been employed by six different companies. In the last one and a half years alone, he either was released or had resigned from three jobs.

Now, let's turn back the clock.

Jonathan and Emily were introduced by a mutual friend and were immediately attracted to each other. Emily thought Jonathan was great looking. He was tall, he jogged five times each week and worked out at least three times a week, he played basketball with his friends on weekends, he had the cutest smile Emily had ever seen. When Jonathan was with her, she felt special. He had also just landed a sales position with a major pharmaceutical company. His starting salary was $2,000 per month, but the average salesman at that company earned more than $50,000 per year, including commission. The territory he was being assigned was one of the best in the company; the man who was retiring from that position had been with the company for 28 years. Her girlfriends thought she was lucky; everyone said that Jonathan was a great catch.

Emily couldn't believe how attentive he was to her. As she told her girlfriends, "He says he just can't stay away from me. He picks me up for lunch every day and we just gaze into each other's eyes and talk about everything. He's so funny, too. Before we know it the time has flown by." Emily told her best friend Sara how she felt when Jonathan kissed her, how he kissed, and what kind of a lover he was. She said "I've never felt like this before. I could stay in bed with him all day." As a matter of fact, they did stay in bed most of the day when Emily slept at Jonathan's apartment.

Everything was perfect. Well, almost. There was only one time that Jonathan made Emily cry — and that, as Emily told Sara, was her fault anyway. Jonathan's car was being serviced and they had made arrangements for him to use her car so he could play basketball with his friends. But Emily had misplaced the keys to her car. Jonathan got really upset and yelled at her. He grabbed her by her shoulders and in doing so he hurt her just a little. He also told her that she was stupid and irresponsible. She had never seen him so mad. But a few hours after he yelled at her, he said he was sorry, and he bought her a rose to make up for it. She thought that was sweet.

When Emily's parents met Jonathan, they liked him, too. He was polite and charming. Emily's father Bill even played basketball with Jonathan in the backyard while Emily and her mom cleaned up the kitchen after lunch when Emily and Jonathan occasionally stopped over for a visit. Sometimes Emily thought her mom Joyce liked Jonathan even more than she did and Joyce told Emily, Jonathan had a knack for saying all the right things. Emily agreed with her mom, although she was kind of embarrassed one time, when after lunch Emily was on the phone with one of her friends and Jonathan said, "Emily, don't just sit there talking on the phone, help your mom clear the table and clean up."

When Jonathan first met Emily he was really turned on by her. He described her to his cousin Ed as having "long, silky blond hair and an incredible body." Jonathan went on to confide, "She makes love better than any girl I've ever dated; she does anything I want her to do while we're in bed and she thinks everything I do is the best. On top of that she thinks I'm really funny and smart. She always looks great and it seems like she has a new outfit every time we go out — although, as I've told her, I think her taste in clothes leaves something to be desired." When Ed asked how she could afford to buy all those clothes, Jonathan brushed it off by saying "her dad probably buys them for her."

There you have it. Jonathan and Emily met, they were attracted to each other, and had fun. They dated for six months and decided to get married. Sounds perfect, huh?

Let's look a little closer at the situation.

When Jonathan and Emily first met, Jonathan had recently dropped out of college after attending classes for one year. His grades at the end of the first year were two Bs, two Cs, and one incomplete: his philosophy professor was not able to issue Jonathan a final grade because he never completed his term paper. Jonathan was a very handsome young man, standing over six feet tall. He was well groomed, well spoken, and was likeable: perfect qualities for his job with the pharmaceutical company, which required him to call on pharmacists in order to encourage them to order the company's products.

Jonathan's future with this pharmaceutical company looked bright. The company thought so, Emily thought so, and so did Emily's parents.

When Emily first met Jonathan she was working for a national discount chain as a clerk, earning $6.50 per hour. She attended a local community college for one semester after graduating from high school, but she didn't especially like school, and all but one of her close friends were already employed full time. As a matter of fact, a couple of friends her age (20) already had babies, and she admittedly had always fantasized about having a baby and being a homemaker like her mom.

Yes, Jonathan was very attentive when they first met, and every day at about noon, regardless of which pharmacists he was scheduled to see, he would travel out of his way to pick Emily up from work so they could have lunch together. Emily was permitted an hour for lunch, but she liked to take longer so she could spend more time with Jonathan. One of her fellow employees covered for her by punching her time card in at 1 p.m. — even if she didn't get back from lunch until 1:30 or so. Both Jonathan and Emily laughed about it. Her employer would never know, and Jonathan could schedule his own appointments, so it was no big deal for him to take that half hour or so to drive to her place of work and enjoy an hour-and-a-half lunch. Besides, they had so much fun together, they'd both miss not being together for lunch.

Jonathan and Emily felt euphoric about their relationship when they first were married. Their physical relationship was terrific. Jonathan said "she would make love to me anytime I wanted it." At first, Emily didn't mind doing that — although she

admitted later that she did to it please him, even though sometimes she didn't feel like it.

■ EUPHORIA WEARS OFF

Jonathan says that their marital problems began when Emily
took responsibility for paying the household bills and generally
didn't pay them on time or even at all. She used the money
Jonathan gave her for that specific purpose to buy clothes for
herself, clothes for Jonathan, or some things that she wanted to
have for the house. She wasn't being totally selfish with the
money, but when it came time to pay the bills, Emily didn't have
any money left.

The first time Jonathan learned about this was three months
after they had been married. He tried to call home from work but
the phone at his home had been disconnected. He couldn't
understand it, because he knew that he had given Emily enough
money to pay all the bills. He called the phone company to ver-
ify payment, but was told there had been no payment. Jonathan
rushed home. Emily was out, but Jonathan found the place
where she kept the unpaid bills and he went through them. What
he discovered astonished him.

Their phone bill was two months late, but it hadn't been shut
off before this because she paid $100 toward it last week. Their
rent payment was one month late. To make matters worse, Emily
had applied for five different credit cards and had been
approved. She had forged Jonathan's name, too. She had
incurred a total debt on those cards of $4,356.

Jonathan was furious.

When Emily arrived home, Jonathan was on his neighbor's
phone calling his office. His boss got on the phone and wanted an
explanation of why he didn't keep the appointment with the
pharmacist he was supposed to see that afternoon. The pharmacist had called and needed certain drugs. When Jonathan didn't
keep his appointment, he called a different drug company. The
pharmacist said this wasn't the first time this sort of thing had

happened. Jonathan's boss wanted to see him first thing the next morning.

As Jonathan was leaving the neighbor's home, he saw Emily's car in the driveway. He just couldn't control himself any longer. He barged into the house, grabbed Emily by the shoulders and slammed her up against the wall and pinned his right index finger against her chest, hurting her to such an extent that she was sure he was bruising her. He began to yell and call her "bitch" and "whore." He said she was irresponsible and lazy and that all she cared about was herself. He said on top of that she was a lousy cook and lover and he couldn't understand why he had ever married her.

Emily didn't know what was wrong until Jonathan began to talk. He said "You've cost me my job, now I don't know how I'll be able to support us. Our telephone is turned off because you were so stupid and selfish that you didn't pay it. And how in hell did you have the nerve to forge my name to credit cards and spend $4,000?" Emily became hysterical, saying, "I was going to tell you — I just kept putting it off because I knew you'd be mad. I'm really sorry that I cost you your job and that I spent all that money. Please forgive me."

That was just the beginning — or should we say more accurately, the end. Emily did try to make up for what she had done. She made it a point to make love to Jonathan anytime he wanted — and then some. She felt desperate to make him happy. She became pregnant within a month or two after that incident. Jonathan was surprised when she told him that she was pregnant, but he had always wanted to have a son. They both thought that having a child would help their marriage.

From that time on, Jonathan went from job to job. He felt that no one he worked for understood how good he was, and that most of the other salesmen he worked with "were not nearly as good-looking or could speak to potential customers with such charm and charisma." Emily remained employed by the discount store, still earning $6.50 per hour, but she had to work a lot of overtime because they had to pay off the debt she had incurred and they couldn't always count on Jonathan's income. They put their baby, Andrea, in day-care while they were both working.

Because of her work schedule, Emily didn't have time to do the laundry as often as she should, so it piled up. Emily didn't seem to have time to clean the kitchen after dinner, because the baby needed so much attention. Jonathan wouldn't help because he thought doing dishes was "woman's work," so the dirty dishes piled up, too.

One evening while Jonathan was watching television, the phone rang. Emily was finally trying to get through some of the wash, so she yelled to Jonathan to get it. He ran to the kitchen and picked up the phone. It was Emily's mother. Within earshot of Emily, Jonathan said, "Emily's trying to clean up this pigsty, but it's so disgusting it'll probably take her two weeks to do it. Can she call you back then? I've got to go, the Knicks and Bulls are playing on TV."

As you might imagine, Emily was horrified and embarrassed, but she was afraid if she made an issue out of it that Jonathan would yell at her and hurt her like he did before. All she said to him was "Did you have to tell my mother that?" Jonathan responded, "It's the truth, isn't it?"

Jonathan wanted to have sex that night. Emily complied, but with her eyes closed tightly so that she could pretend that she didn't have to see or feel him. Jonathan disgusted her. According to what Jonathan told his friends, Emily was the laziest, dumbest, most irresponsible woman he could have ever married; they were deeply in debt because of her spending and forging his signature on credit cards; and he keeps losing jobs because of her stupidity.

■ TIME TO TAKE ACCOUNT

Now let's look at Jonathan and Emily from our perspective. Remember, we're not hypnotized by the infatuation of being in love, like they were. We're being objective about some pretty important aspects of each of their lives, and as we're analyzing their relationship from *our* perspective, we don't have to take into consideration input (wanted or unwanted) from family and friends.

Let's start with Jonathan. Here's what we have learned from things he said, as well as things we observed:

1. Jonathan dropped out of college after attending classes for only one year, and he received an incomplete grade in philosophy because he never completed his term paper — a very good indication that he has trouble completing the things he starts.

2. Although Jonathan had a really terrific job opportunity, he acted irresponsibly by taking Emily out to lunch every day, which — taking travel time into consideration — cut two hours out of his eight-hour workday.

3. Jonathan encouraged Emily to take longer than the hour she had for lunch and stood by quietly while she cheated her employer by having a co-worker punch her in on the time clock at 1 p.m. even though she often didn't return from lunch until 1:30 p.m.

4. When Emily lost the keys to her car, Jonathan yelled at her and was verbally abusive, calling her stupid and irresponsible. He was critical of the clothes Emily wore. He openly criticized her in front of her parents on more than one occasion. In general, it is obvious he didn't worry about undermining Emily's self image.

5. Jonathan thought saying he was sorry and bringing Emily a rose would excuse his abusive behavior and that he would be forgiven.

6. Jonathan thinks it's a woman's job to remove the dishes from the table. He opted to play basketball with Emily's father when he and Emily visited with her parents rather than first helping Emily's mother.

7. Jonathan thought physical violence was acceptable

behavior, as he demonstrated when he grabbed Emily by the shoulders.

Now, let's take a look at Emily:

1. At least in the early stages of her relationship with Jonathan, Emily was satisfied with her high school education, and working as a clerk for $4.75 per hour.
2. Emily often wore a new outfit; she spent a fair amount of money on clothes.
3. Emily was dishonest. She allowed a co-worker to punch in her time card at work even though she hadn't returned from lunch.
4. We know from her being on the telephone while her mom was cleaning up after lunch that she had a tendency to allow others to do her work.

So, who screwed up? They both did. Here's how.

Emily treated Jonathan's abusiveness too lightly. She rarely allowed herself to feel the pain of hearing him yell at her or call her names. She didn't allow herself to acknowledge that physical abuse of *any* kind is unacceptable behavior. She continued to be with him even though he embarrassed her in front of her parents by telling her that she was lazy. She continued to be with him even though he cheated his employer by spending working hours with her. She continued to be with him even though he thought nothing of leaving dirty dishes on the table and going out to play basketball. She continued to be with him even though he commented negatively on how she looked by criticizing the clothes she wore.

In short, Emily accepted Jonathan's negative behavior and placed more emphasis on his great looks, attentiveness, terrific lovemaking, and the fact that her family and friends thought Jonathan was wonderful.

Jonathan, too, ignored the fact that Emily was dishonest with her employer by allowing her co-worker to punch her time card even though she hadn't yet returned from lunch. He didn't examine the implications of her excessive spending habits, nor did he weigh the importance of Emily's sitting idly by while her mom did her work. And finally, Jonathan failed to realize that Emily was very young: that, for now, she was satisfied with a high school education, earning $6.50 an hour, and having babies like her other friends. He failed to realize that eventually — no matter how satisfied she thought she would be staying home, taking care of the house, and raising children — she would feel confined and resentful. She would not feel fulfilled. And Jonathan would get the brunt of the anger Emily felt toward herself for allowing herself to end up in that situation.

■ INTERPRET BEHAVIOR AS A PROMISE

From the very first moment of our initial contact with someone, we begin to make promises — just like Jonathan and Emily began making promises to each other from the first moment they met. We make promises not only from the things we say but also from the things we do.

We must remain aware that if the person with whom we are establishing a relationship continues to exhibit negative characteristics, their behavior should be interpreted as their "promise" to continually exhibit those negative characteristics. When we ignore their promise to be exactly the same after marriage as before, we have no one to blame but ourselves if we can't tolerate their behavior. Needless to say, it's impossible to be best friends with someone whose behavior you can't tolerate, even though that behavior may have been only that which was promised in the first place.

To be your partner's best friend, you must also remain aware that once you *make* a promise, you must try not to break it. Imagine how peaceful you could be in your partner's presence if you knew what to expect from them because they were always consistent in their behavior and temperament. Your feeling of trust towards your partner stems from being certain that your partner's behavior will be consistent. Being truly peaceful comes from being able to trust. You have to be careful to accurately acknowledge to yourself what your partner is promising before you make a commitment to be their best friend for life. You have to be certain that you can live with their promised behavior and temperament so you can trust your partner and, as a result of that trust, feel peaceful while living your life with them.

CHAPTER 2

BEING TEACHABLE

*W*hat does it mean when someone says that another person is "teachable?" It means that they are being sufficiently open to a softly stated suggestion of how they can approach a situation differently. We're not talking about someone altering behavior in order to be accepted, as we were when we spoke about being controlled. We're talking about changing your behavior because you believe your behavior needed changing after reflecting on the suggestion.

Let's see how this might work.

She says: "Why did you find it necessary to share so much information about your business affairs with the couple we were with tonight?"

He says: What's the big deal, we'll probably never see them again."

She says: "Honey, you're sharing too much information about our business with people we don't even know. Please don't do it again."

He knows he shared too much information. He's slightly embarrassed because she pointed it out to him. His tendency was to be defensive. He knew, however, that she was right. The next time they were out with another couple, he was more careful not to share too much information about himself, and instead directed the conversation toward the couple they were with. *That's* being teachable.

Here's another situation.

It's Sunday afternoon and, although he would rather be elsewhere, he went with her to her parent's home because he knew she didn't want to go alone. While he's there, he overhears her telling her mom and dad that the two of them are looking for a new car. He knows she wants to share the information with them partially because she wants them to think, "They must be doing well if they're buying a new car." He wishes she hadn't told them yet, because he's not sure his credit application will be approved; he's been late in making some of his payments recently. He doesn't want to be embarrassed if that application is not approved.

This is how the conversation goes on the way home:

He says: "Honey, I really wish you hadn't told your parents about the car yet. I'm going to feel embarrassed if our credit's not approved."

She says: "Our credit will be approved, won't it? Besides, we can buy ap used car if our credit's not approved, rather than a new one."

He says: "But I'll be embarrassed."

From that point on, she's being teachable if she waits before she shares certain information with her parents.

Now, consider similar conversations with a couple who are not being conscious of being their partner's best friend, and who — by the harshness of their words — reduce the chance that their partner can be, or is willing to be, teachable.

He shares too much personal financial information with the couple they're with on Saturday night. They drop them off at their home, and then the "conversation" begins:

She says, "Damn it! Why did you have to tell them your entire life story? You're so stupid sometimes. You tell people things like that so they'll think you're a big man."

If she phrases the message with that tone, you can be sure he'll react much differently. A statement phrased like that induces "shrinkage" in a man as much as a dip in a cold pool.

It's the same when he explains to her why he doesn't want her parents to know they're looking for a new car until his credit is approved. The message he's trying to deliver is going to be difficult for her to accept if he attacks her with sentences like "You always have to tell your parents our personal business. You act like a little girl still seeking their approval."

If you want your partner to be teachable, you cannot phrase your message in a manner that immediately raises a red flag. Don't start your message with a statement that will cause them to feel intimidated or defensive.

CHAPTER 3

HOW PARENTS
PLAY A PART

*W*e've all heard the terms "Mommy's boy" or "Daddy's little girl." Those ages-old labels hint at the influence our parents have had upon our character, our set of beliefs, our every behavior — whether good or bad. Find out about your partner's relationships with their parents — and how your partner's parents related to each other — and you've gained a huge insight into what's going on inside your partner's head at any given moment, and why they act the way they do.

■ HIS MOM WAS HIS BEST FRIEND

If a man's mom was his best friend when he was a child, undoubtedly he likes and respects women and treats them accordingly. Since he loved cuddling with her, he will like cuddling with you. He'll feel comfortable expressing his feelings, since he probably did so with his mother. He'll enjoy doing things for you, since his mom's loving smile and hugs were his rewards when he did things for her. Most likely he'll also be more in touch with his feminine side, which should enable him to appreciate even the smallest things you do for him — and help him to anticipate your needs. As you might have already guessed, if he had a good relationship with his mom, he has a big head start toward being Mr. Right.

On the other hand, if his mom was critical of him and controlling, he might not like or respect women, and as such he most likely treats them accordingly. He may also be critical and exhibit controlling behavior, too. He will probably be overly defensive to any criticism and he may not always tell you the truth, because he probably lied to his mom in order to avoid her wrath. He may not be gentle and affectionate with you because she may not have been open to him being that way with her. If she was physically abusive, he may also be physically abusive. He may also do things that are intended to hurt you, such as comparing you to other women.

Notwithstanding the foregoing, it would be grossly unfair of me to suggest that you rule out any man who did not have a good relationship with his mother. There are a great number of men in this world who would acknowledge and respect your perspective (even if they may not agree with it), keep promises, work hard at their jobs, and are responsible about paying bills — even if they did not have a healthy relationship with their mothers. In other words, there are many men out there who were raised by controlling, manipulative mothers who are good men and are teachable. If you choose a man who didn't have that wonderful relationship, be absolutely sure he's teachable and madly in love with you. If he is, it's not too late to teach him to be sensitive and to be in touch with your need to be respected and appreciated — especially if he understands and is able to acknowledge those parts of him that haven't yet been developed. Nevertheless, date him for a long time before you make a commitment.

■ HIS DAD WAS HIS MOM'S BEST FRIEND, TOO

If a man's dad was his mom's best friend, he has had the experience of watching another man treat a women with respect and consideration. As such, he probably believes that things like helping with the housework, making the children school lunches, and driving the kids to school is not only acceptable but expected behavior.

On the other hand, if his dad was physically and verbally abusive to his mother, he may have identified with that negative behavior pattern. He most likely will believe he's right about everything and won't think your perspective is worth listening to. If so, you'll recognize this behavior quickly the first time he says things like, "You're stupid and don't know anything," "You're lazy," or "Can't you do anything right?" Take heed now: AVOID THIS MAN. He is *not* your Mr. Right — although he certainly he thinks he is!

■ DADDY'S BOY

I'd like to tell you about a couple for whom, as this book was being written, I was mediating a dissolution of marriage. Obviously, I'm not going to use their true names, but for my purposes here, I'll refer to them as Barbara and Gary. Gary grew up in a home where his father was verbally and physically abusive to Gary's mom; Gary did not have a warm relationship with his mom either. His father was very much a disciplinarian and he made Gary "toe the line," so to speak. When Gary married Barbara, who is sensitive, in touch, communicative, and loving, she had a three-year-old little girl. We'll call her Sharon.

Gary, you should know, is conscientious, responsible, and there's nothing lazy about him when it comes to meeting responsibilities around the house. He's also extremely good-looking, with a terrific sense of humor. Gary has never hit Barbara and neither of them have ever had an affair. At the time they got in touch with me, they had been married 14 years.

When Gary first called us, he said that he and Barbara were still living together, but that Barbara had filed for dissolution of marriage. He wanted to reconcile the marriage, although he admitted that he had walked out of therapy after the third session. He expressed hope that as a result of mediation their lines of communication might reopen and Barbara might be willing to consider reconciliation and counseling. During our first phone conversation, I asked him why he thought Barbara didn't want to be married to him any longer and he responded, "It's hard to teach this cowboy new tricks." I assumed he meant that she wanted him to change his behavior and he couldn't do it. I suggested he go to a bookstore and buy one of my little black books entitled *A Man's Guide To Being A Woman's Best Friend*. I told him that after taking the six or seven minutes it would take him to read it, that he might be able to identify the *real* reason Barbara wanted to dissolve the marriage.

Gary brought the book with him to his first appointment (sometimes I meet with each party individually first to see if both of them are open to mediating a resolution to the issues of the dissolution of their marriage), and I asked him if he now understood why Barbara couldn't be married to him any longer. He said he did.

Gary revealed that although he did about 70 per cent of the things that were identified in the book, and then added that he was a lot like his dad, that he loved his dad, and he was sure that the way his dad did things was right. Clearly he identified with everything about his dad — who, it turned out, thought he was right about everything and who rarely listened to Gary's mom's perspective. Gary didn't think he could change or that he even *wanted* to change, because he was convinced that his father was correct in the way he did everything. When I asked him if he loved Barbara and could change his behavior if that was the only way she would remain married to him, he wept openly.

Do you understand why he wept like this? Think about it for a moment.

Gary wept openly because he *wished* he could change his behavior — but he couldn't *allow* himself to because it would have meant that he was abandoning his father's belief system and consequently he felt he would be abandoning his father as well. He viewed himself as "Daddy's boy," and to think about severing that tie was more than he could bear.

About a week later I met with Barbara. She confirmed Gary's own assessment. She still wished he could change, but didn't think that was possible. She believed that he was too pig-headed to change, just like his dad. She said that she didn't want to consider reconciling the marriage: she had been hurt too much and was too afraid to allow herself to be vulnerable any longer. No fairy-tale ending here, I'm afraid.

What can be learned from the sad experience of Gary and Barbara's failed marriage? For a man to have a good start in understanding how to be a woman's best friend, it is helpful for him to have had a father who didn't think he had to be right all the time about everything. If a man has seen his father listen and be sensitive to his mother's perspective and sometimes accept her perspective, that man most likely will do the same with the woman he marries. He more than likely will be teachable, too. On the other hand, if a man like Gary has been raised to believe that men are all-powerful and all-knowing, then even though that man may be wonderful in many other aspects of his life, it may make being married to him intolerable.

■ HER DAD WAS HER BEST FRIEND

A woman who has not had a good relationship with her dad in a sense feels that she has been abandoned by her dad. A little girl is supposed to be the apple of her daddy's eye. We think of her sitting in her dad's lap, being hugged and kissed by him; we think of him giving in to her whims and wishes because he's so crazy about her. Women who have been yelled at, criticized by, and even hit by their dads are extremely sensitive to any man treating them the same way. Any such behavior by a man will trigger the feeling that she is being abandoned.

A woman who has had a good relationship with her dad expects to be treated the same way by the man who professes to love her. As such, she will react negatively if she is not treated with sensitivity and respect and provided with lots of affection. She clearly is her daddy's little girl, and will be so even as an adult. If a man who is with such a woman doesn't feel secure about himself, and if he perceives her undying devotion for her dad as competition, that feeling and perception can cause him to feel that whatever he does is not good enough. Too often he feels that she is comparing him to her dad, and because he may at times feel somewhat insecure, he will feel that he pales by comparison.

What's a guy to do? If he has a relationship with a woman who has had a *good* relationship with her dad, he has huge shoes to fill. If he has a relationship with a woman who feels *abandoned* by her dad, she may be so afraid to be abandoned again that it may make it difficult for her to trust any man. So which one is Ms Right?

I believe *every* woman has potential to be Ms. Right — if a guy can be patient enough to earn her trust. She will be Ms Right if her partner understands how she felt growing up with a father who she felt didn't love her, and that partner loves her and helps her to feel secure in their relationship. If a man listens to a woman without interrupting, if he never criticizes her, if he treats her as his equal and doesn't patronize her, if he keeps every promise, and if he holds her, touches her face gently, and says words like "I love you — be safe today, honey," most women will respond positively — unless, for whatever reason, they simply cannot be satisfied at that time of their life.

If a woman had a poor relationship with her dad, she can still be Ms. Right, but a man must help her to be aware of her tendency to feel that every man will abandon her, like she was abandoned by her dad. Her partner must gently help her to understand that she should try not to consider every little emotional outburst to be abandonment.

He needs to help her verbalize how she felt as a little girl when her father ignored her when she wanted to tell him something about school or her dance lessons. He needs to help her express how she felt when her father criticized her clothes, or made her feel bad about herself when she was a little too pudgy or a little too thin. Her partner needs to maintain a heightened awareness of how she felt. He needs to be patient with her when she feels a little insecure.

She, however, needs to be able to recognize the difference between emotional abuse and slightly insensitive behavior. She cannot let herself be subjected to emotional abuse again.

If she had a great relationship with her dad, Ms. Right is a woman who is aware that her dad will always have a special place in her heart: a place of special memories and feelings like none other provided by any other man. She must remain aware that her tendency will be to compare every man to her father, and that she sets herself up for disappointment if a man doesn't compare favorably. She must not compare a man with whom she falls in love with her dad. She must allow herself to open the door to another, *different* place in her heart for her partner. A place where *new* special memories and feelings are stored. A place where her partner feels comfortable knowing that he's loved too, and where he doesn't have to compete with her dad to be accepted by her.

■ HER DAD WAS HER MOM'S BEST FRIEND, TOO

If a woman's dad was her mom's best friend, she grew up identifying with a woman who responded in positive ways to being loved. She identified with a woman who conveyed the message to her man that he was trusted and that she liked the way he was and didn't need to change. She identified with a woman who let her man know that his best was good enough and understood the pressure he felt to be the primary wage earner. She identified with a woman who understood that men, in sometimes too many ways, will always be little boys — needing to be told that they are big and strong, needing to be babied when they are sick, and needing to be able to show off some of the time and talk about himself and his work too much of the time. She identified with a woman who wanted to love her guy because she felt loved all of the time herself.

CHAPTER 4

YOUR PARTNER'S MIND
IS YOUR PLAYGROUND

$\mathcal{W}$e often hear someone who is in love say "he makes me laugh," or "one of the reasons I love her is because she's funny." Do we say those words because our partner tells a good joke or tries to be a comedian? Or do we say those words because our partner is able to tune into our mind and play with it? It's the latter.

Undeniably, at first blush it's a difficult concept to grasp. Frankly, your partner and you have to be in love or falling in love for it to happen. It happens when there is a connection between your mind and your partner's mind. Your partner is able to make your mind their playground when they are able to link their mind to yours to watch it work, to hear its thoughts, and to respond to those thoughts. What's funny or what makes you laugh is not what's said. What's funny is that you recognize your partner was able to watch what was going on inside your mind. You know your partner has "tuned in," and you love it. It tickles you. You allow your mind — even if it's just for a moment — to link up with your partner's mind, and your attention is distracted from the chaos of the day. Even the thought of your partner being able to do that makes you smile or even laugh. It's not that your partner is so darn funny. To *you* they're funny. Believe me, no one else would get it.

Is this as important as your partner being teachable or as important as some of the other things discussed earlier? Absolutely. In some ways it's even more important. You see, it's this ability to "link up" their mind with yours that allows your partner to anticipate your needs, to feel your mood without asking about it, to be sensitive to those things about which you may be feeling self-conscious or anxious. It's your partner taking time off from whatever they're doing to be with *you* — and only you. It may be the best way that your partner "makes love" to you. It's your partner making love to your mind. It's the best kind of foreplay. It can't replace sex … but it's a heck of a good replacement while you're still wearing your clothes!

CHAPTER 5

SO JUST WHO *IS*
THAT SPECIAL SOMEONE?

*F*ar too often, couples fall in love with the feeling of being in love. They overlook the fact that the process of living life daily is a huge struggle for all of us, requiring us to dedicate every ounce of our strength, discipline, and emotional stability to the process of simply surviving. If we permit ourselves to enter into a long-term relationship with someone who is not nurturing, responsible, honest, and considerate, the struggle to survive becomes too great. We eventually shut down emotionally in order to block the pain inflicted by that very person we wanted to love and trust, and we begin to pass through life as if in a dream. Inevitably, though, we awaken from that dream and begin to express and project the anger we feel at ourselves for marrying this person onto our spouse.

Mr./Ms. Right is a person you respect for all of the reasons we feel respect for someone. It's a person who recognizes the importance of accepting an equal share of responsibility for all the things we each have to do everyday, including being jointly responsible for their children. It's a person who has a strong personality, but who doesn't have a need to dominate. It's a person who is comfortable giving in to your wishes without an argument, and who recognizes that it's not important to win an argument. It's a person who compromises — but not *too* easily — when they feel strongly about an issue.

Mr./Ms. Right is also sensitive to a partner's need for personal growth, and is secure enough to encourage that growth. It's someone who believes that a success for their partner is a success for them, too. It's someone with whom a partner can establish a balance of power, and who understands the meaning of the words "share and share alike" as they relate to all aspects of living life with another person.

When choosing that person who you want to be your best friend in life, you must maintain your highest level of awareness. You must not overlook warning signs (as did Jonathan and Emily). You must not allow yourself to be with a person who cannot acknowledge their failings, who does not try hard everyday to improve, who gets discouraged easily and gives up when at first they don't succeed. You must maintain your awareness level and consciously weigh the positive against the negative. You must allow yourself to consciously examine which negative personality characteristics or "baggage" you are willing and able to accept, and which you are not. You must not fool yourself into thinking that once you're married, the negative characteristics will disappear.

And last but certainly not least, you must not succumb to the feeling of being *in* love *with* love. Only enter into a marital relationship when you are fully able to commit yourself to being your partner's best friend for life.

PART
TWO

The Passkey
to the Door
of Your Past

CHAPTER 6

TRUST ENOUGH
TO GIVE THEM THE KEY

*M*any of us are afraid that if we allow another person to *really* get to know us, they may not like us. We are also afraid that once they *do* know us, they will know the things that can hurt us the most. Most of us, at one time or another, have been hurt by a parent, another family member, a lover, or a close friend.

The fear we have felt and the hurt we have experienced tend to make each of us wary of trusting any other person with the key that unlocks the door to our past. It makes us wary of allowing any other person to see into every nook and cranny of our being. They will see our imperfections. They will see where we are most vulnerable. They will see those things of which we are most ashamed. They'll see those things of which we are most afraid. They will be able to hurt us once they know everything about us.

It sounds scary.

It is scary.

On the other hand, if you *don't* allow the person who you have decided will be your partner through life to know you, then you don't allow them the chance to know all the things about you that there are to love. You don't allow them to have the knowledge that will enable them to be there for you when you are feeling weak, to help you enhance your strengths, or to encourage you to reach for your dreams. You don't allow them to help you fight your demons. You don't allow them to be your partner.

In case you haven't noticed, survival itself is fairly hard work. To succeed at providing ourselves and our families with a healthy, happy, financially secure life is even harder. We all look for ways to earn more money, to be happier and healthier, or to feel more secure in our relationships. It's probably one of the reasons you're reading this book. In these words, you're hoping to find some insight into how you can help to make your relationship better. Navigating through the course of life is difficult. It's even more difficult if we have to do it alone.

By giving your partner — your love — the passkey to your past, not only do you provide them with valuable knowledge that will enable them to know and understand you better, but you also convey the message that you trust them. Hopefully your openness with them will lead to their openness with you. If you're in an "open" relationship like this, neither of you will find it necessary to hide anything from each other. For example, you won't mind accepting responsibility for a mistake, because your partner knows you've made some mistakes before. You can go ahead and express your fear of failure, because you probably have already shared not only your successes but your failures with your partner. You can cry openly and not be embarrassed by it. You will feel more comfortable being in your partner's presence because you can let your defenses down when you are with them. You won't have to pretend that you're "all that."

Giving your partner the passkey to your past also helps them to understand you better, and to have special insights into you that very few — if any — others have. It allows them to be perceptive if they choose to be tuned in.

CHAPTER 7

LEARNING ABOUT YOUR PAST
HELPS YOUR PARTNER
TO UNDERSTAND YOU

*I*magine that you weren't feeling well for about a month and couldn't pinpoint the problem. You were tired much of the time, you had a slight headache, and, although you didn't have a fever, you had chills now and then. You want to make an appointment with a doctor, but your doctor retired about six months ago, and you don't know who to call. A friend refers you to their doctor and you call to make an appointment. When you arrive at the doctor's office, the secretary gives you a medical history form to complete so that the doctor will have a better idea of what childhood illnesses you've had as well as a history of your specific medical conditions. The nurse weighs you and takes your temperature and blood pressure. The doctor asks questions about your medical history, examines you, takes a chest X-ray, runs blood tests, perhaps an electrocardiogram and stress test, and may even recommend that other tests be done.

The object of all this, of course, is to generate as much medical knowledge about you as possible so that the doctor can better understand why you're not feeling well. It would leave too much to chance if the doctor tried to help you without knowing as many details of your past and present medical and psychological history as possible.

Now imagine that you're having lunch with a friend at a restaurant and an acquaintance of your friend walks up to your table to say hello. You're introduced, and immediately you feel attracted to this person — and you sense they're attracted to you as well. When you're again alone with your friend, you ask some questions about your friend's acquaintance and then say you'd like to go out with them. A date is eventually scheduled. Let's further imagine that you fall in love, date for a long time, and eventually decide to marry this person.

Your new doctor needed to know your complete medical history and had to conduct a thorough physical examination in order to understand why you were not feeling well. Similarly, you must know as much about your partner's childhood, teenage, and young adult years — and the effect family members, friends, and experiences have had on your partner — in order for you to have the awareness level you'll need in order to be your partner's best friend. It is very difficult for you to interpret your partner's behavior, understand your partner's fears, or be sensitive and in touch with your partner's thought processes if you don't know everything about the life of your love.

The rest of this section of *Best Friends Forever* will give you an idea of the type of information you should know about your partner — as well as an example or two of what you might glean from the information. It is by no means everything you should know about your partner. Remember — the more you learn, the more you will be able to understand the person with whom you've fallen in love. (Access my website — *www.bestfriendsforever.com* — and download "Personal Reflections" if you want to see a complete guide to learning everything about your partner.)

■ WHAT IF YOUR PARTNER WON'T OPEN UP TO YOU?

If your partner doesn't freely open up to you, you need to maintain an even greater, heightened level of awareness about your partner. Draw conclusions about their past from consistent behavior patterns. Commit those conclusions to memory as if they have been shared insights from your partner, and, ever so gently, once in a while, make a soft reference to "what must have happened" when a behavior pattern repeats itself. Perhaps then, your partner may begin to share more of their deepest thoughts and feelings.

It'll take time. Be patient. Your partner must feel safe with you before they'll share everything.

■ CHILDHOOD MEMORIES

Ask your partner to let their mind drift back as far as it will go. Ask them to picture their very first memory. Ask them to describe the significance of that memory, if any. Then ask them to reflect on their first traumatic experience. Have them describe the event in as much detail as they wish, including where they were and with whom they were involved. Ask them to describe what impact or significance that trauma had on their life.

Ask them to tell you how old they were when this traumatic experience occurred. How did this experience make them feel? Angry, sad, abandoned, confused? Ask them to tell you who helped them deal with this crisis and how that person helped them.

If, for example, the traumatic experience they describe was that their father died from either lung cancer or a heart attack when they were young, they may have felt abandoned by the parent who died. If you smoke cigarettes or are overweight, your partner may be afraid that *you* will abandon them, also. This fear of abandonment may cause them to over-react to anything you do that even *slightly* seems reminiscent of abandonment. In fact, they are so afraid of being abandoned that they may even undermine positive aspects of your relationship — in effect abandoning *you* before you abandon them.

■ HOME AND NEIGHBORHOOD

Did your partner live in a home, apartment, or mobile home? Was the home in an upper-, middle-, or lower-class neighborhood? What was their favorite room in the house? Did they share a room with a brother or sister? How did they feel about their home and neighborhood? When your partner thinks back to their childhood home and neighborhood, do they wish that they could live in a neighborhood and home just like the one in which they grew up?

Did your partner's parents earn a very good living, have an average income, or did they struggle to make ends meet?

If your partner was friends with kids who lived in an upper- or upper- to middle-class neighborhood, but lived in a lower- or middle- to lower-class neighborhood, did they feel embarrassed by their home? If so, it might explain, for example, why they feel driven to work so many long hours, or are inclined to put pressure on you to earn more money.

■ CHILDHOOD RELATIONSHIP WITH EACH PARENT (INDIVIDUALLY)

Were your partner's parents open, caring, distant, or strained? Were they kind, gentle, abusive, difficult to talk to, or controlling? Did your partner think that their parents loved or did not love them? Did they love, like, or dislike their parents? Did your partner's parents make them feel worthy, unworthy, useless? Did their parents say that they were smart, good, hard-working, sensitive, handsome, pretty, lazy, stupid, bad? Were they critical of them? Did their parents yell at them? Did their parents physically or sexually abuse them?

If your partner feels unworthy of being loved because their parents yelled at them, physically or sexually abused them, or said that they were stupid or lazy, they may not feel confident or secure about themselves. They may be very sensitive to any similar behavior on your part, and they may shut down emotionally in order to prevent you from hurting them the way their parents hurt them. Your unkind actions or words may bring back the feelings of pain your partner felt when their parents did or said something unkind. If you are aware of how your partner's parents made them feel by their behavior and choice of words, you will be more sensitive to how *your* behavior and choice of words will make your partner feel.

What was the most common relationship problem your partner had with their parents? Were there any long-term consequences from this relationship problem? As your partner grew older, did the relationship with their parents remain the same, become closer, or grow distant? Did your partner feel that they got enough love from their parents?

If your partner was not openly hugged and kissed by their parents, they might need much more hugging and kissing to feel loved. It also might help to explain why your partner doesn't feel comfortable showing you or your children much affection. If this is the case, you might pay particular attention to sharing your love and affection often. You might also help your partner to be more affectionate with you and be more patient until they are more comfortable doing so.

Does your partner think that they would be a different person today if their relationship with their parents had been something other than what it was? What do they think is the most important thing a parent can do for their child? What do they think is important for a parent to understand? What do they wish their parents had done differently?

Your partner might be harboring some anger towards their parents. If this is true, it might help to explain how your partner acts when they are in their presence. You might also note some overcompensation when it comes to your own children. For example, if your partner's parents never came to their basketball games or dance recitals, your partner might insist on being at every one of your children's special events — and will begin to resent you if you choose not to go to these events.

■ PARENTS' RELATIONSHIP WITH EACH OTHER

Did your partner's father treat their mother as though he respected her and thought she was intelligent? Did he listen to her without interrupting? Did he keep the promises he made to her? Did he emotionally or physically abuse her? Did he cater to her needs? Did their father help their mother with work around the house? Did he call her when he was going to be home later than expected? Does your partner remember their father kissing and hugging their mother often? Did your partner's father include their mother in major decisions, or did he make them himself? What was the most important thing your partner learned from their parents' relationship with each other?

The primary reason that you should know — as early in your relationship as possible — as much as you can about your partner's parents' relationship with each other, is that you will know whether your partner identifies with a relationship that was positive and nurturing or one that was negative and perhaps even abusive. You'll be able to determine what they expect from both you and themselves as it relates to your relationship with each other.

■ RELATIONSHIP WITH SIBLINGS

Was the relationship with your partner's siblings warm and loving, competitive, hateful, or fun? What did they like most about their siblings? What did they like least? Was your partner the sibling who had the most talent scholastically, athletically, or musically? Were they envious of the talents of their siblings? Did your partner wish that they were more like their siblings? If so, ask them to explain how they wished they were different.

How did your partner's parents treat them as compared to how their parents treated their siblings? If your partner feels that they were often compared to their siblings, how did that comparison make them feel?

If, for example, one or both of your partner's parents compared them to their siblings, and that comparison made your partner feel less worthy, you'll need to remember to be careful about comparing them to anyone else. Their negative reaction to such comparison could be much greater than you might expect, because they may not be simply reacting to your comment, but reacting to their parents' past comparisons of them to their siblings.

■ RELATIONSHIP WITH GRANDPARENTS

Ask your partner to tell you — to the best of their knowledge — the name, dates of birth, and places of birth of their maternal and paternal grandparents. Was their relationship with their grandparents close or did they have little or no contact? What did their grandparents do for a living before they retired? Did their grandparents play an important role in your partner's life? What was the one thing that they liked to do best with their grandparents? What was the one thing they learned from each of them?

What is their favorite story about their grandfathers? What was the thing they liked best about visiting their grandfathers' houses? Ask them to think about their grandfathers and grandmothers and try to describe what characteristics that their grandparents had that are similar to their own characteristics.

Ask them to tell you when their grandparents health began to deteriorate. What age were their grandparents when they died? Ask your partner to tell you the cause of each of their deaths.

It is important to remember that some of the questions you'll be asking throughout this "exercise" are purely to know more about your partner's life and what they liked or didn't like, and may not be asked to glean any specific information. From asking these questions about their grandparents, though, you might learn how they feel about the importance of being close with family. You also may learn about some aspect of your partner's health that may be hereditary, which you may need to pay attention to as your partner ages.

■ GRADE SCHOOL, JUNIOR HIGH SCHOOL, AND HIGH SCHOOL YEARS

What were your partner's earliest feelings about school? Were they positive or negative? What impact did those feelings have upon their performance in school? Did teachers, subjects, or anything else specific contribute to the way they felt? In which subject did they excel or do poorly? What grades did your partner get? Were they prepared each day when they went to school? Were they satisfied with their performance?

Did your partner's parents support them and help them feel good about their performance in school, or were they not supportive and made them feel badly about themselves? Did they feel as though they were as smart as, smarter than most of, or not as smart as their classmates? What were your partner's favorite school-related activities? Were their school years filled with anxiety, or were they happy and content? As your partner looks back on those school years, what do they wish that they had done that they didn't do?

If your partner was satisfied with their performance in school, if their memories of their school years were happy rather than filled with anxiety, and if your partner's parents were supportive rather than critical, they probably felt confident and good about themselves. They probably think they are intelligent. That feeling of confidence may have carried over to their young adult and adult years, and they probably have continued to build on that solid base of success and good feelings about themselves.

On the other hand, if your partner was dissatisfied with, or even ashamed of, their performance in school, and had negative feelings about themselves, you may notice either a tendency to overcompensate with their desire to succeed, or you may notice that they have a tendency to feel insecure because they lack a good self-image. Your partner may even feel that they have nothing of interest and importance to say; you could hear them say something like "I'm so stupid" when they make a mistake or don't understand something.

It's important for you to be able to understand what your partner really means or wants from you when they say something like "I'm so stupid." They mean "I don't feel good about my intelligence level." They're asking you to say something comforting like "You don't have to understand everything, honey —

you do so many things well that there's no reason for you to be intelligent about politics [or sports, or whatever your partner may have been referring to at that moment]." By knowing how your partner perceived themselves as a child and how their parents, teachers, and friends made them feel about themselves, you will have a greater understanding of how you need to respond to be your partner's best friend.

■ APPEARANCE

What was the thing about your partner's appearance that bothered them the most? Did they think that they were good looking, just mediocre, or not attractive at all?

If your partner didn't think that they were attractive or if they disliked something specific about their looks, they may on occasion say something like, "I look fat," "I hate my hair," or "my complexion is terrible." If you are aware, for example, that your partner once felt self-conscious about their weight, and you heard them say "I look fat," it wouldn't be such a bad idea to respond by walking over to them, holding their face in your hands, kissing their lips softly, and saying something like "Maybe *you* think so, but *I* think you're gorgeous and I love you."

Similarly, if you know that your partner was especially sensitive to being overweight as a child because their mother or father was overly critical of them (or because other children made fun of them), what they would really be saying if they said "I look fat" is "Help me to feel that I'm worthy even if I *am* overweight, and let me know that you love me." By knowing that your partner may have been ridiculed as a child because of their weight, you've gained an important level of insight.

■ GENERAL RECOLLECTIONS

Ask your partner to complete the following statements:
- My proudest moment during my childhood was when...
- During my childhood and teenage years, the one thing I did best was...

- My saddest moment during my childhood was when…
- My lucky break came when I…
- My biggest problem during my childhood and teenage years was…
- During my teenage and young adult years, one constant concern of mine was…
- Goals which I set for myself as a teenager were…
- During my teenage years my worst habits were…
- During my teenage years my best traits were…
- One story that I'm a little embarrassed to relate is…
- Overall, I'd consider my childhood and teenage years to be…

■ LIFE-ALTERING EVENTS

Ask your partner to look back at their life during their childhood and adolescent years and describe one event that they feel changed or had a significant impact on their life.

■ HINDSIGHT

Ask your partner to answer the following question:

If you could reinvent the circumstances of your childhood and adolescent years — and *yourself* during that time of your life — what would be different?

■ LIFE AFTER HIGH SCHOOL

After high school, did your partner begin work, move from their parent's home, join the military, travel, etc.? Was the decision an easy or difficult one to make? Did they make the decision with the help of their parents, friends, and other close family members or friends, or did they make the decision by themselves? Did they go to college or decide not to go to college? Did they have any regrets about the decisions they made at that time?

If your partner went to college, which college did they attend? At what point in their college career did they choose a major course of study? What factors did they take into consideration when choosing their course of study? Does your partner consider their years in college to be productive or unproductive? Do they have any regrets as to their choices?

There are some things that you can learn about your partner that will enable you to better understand their thought processes. If, for example, you learn that your partner respects and appreciates input from other people when they are faced with having to make a difficult decision, you'll feel more comfortable expressing your thoughts when they are facing a major life decision. On the other hand, if you learn that they are used to making all of their decisions alone without input from others, you may be slightly more careful before expressing your thoughts.

However, if your partner has regrets about some of their decisions that may have been made without advice or input from others, and they have openly shared their regrets with you, you may tactfully be able to remind them about those regrets. If they feel a little defensive you might try offering alternative ways to approach a major decision.

■ PHYSICAL FITNESS AND HEALTH

As a young adult, did your partner concentrate on maintaining good physical fitness? Did they exercise daily, a few times a week, or less frequently? Did they consider their health to be excellent, good, fair, or poor? Did they contract colds frequently? How often did they go to a doctor for a physical examination? Were they ever hospitalized for an illness? Is there a chronic physical ailment they have that gives them problems?

Do they have a history of difficulty controlling their weight? Have they found it necessary to diet frequently? Is there any food or medicine to which your partner is allergic? As a young adult, did they smoke cigarettes, or abuse alcohol or drugs?

It's important to be able to anticipate your partner's needs so that you can help them whenever possible. It's also important to consciously maintain an awareness of their physical well-being so that you can be immediately available to help if they need your help. If you know, for example, that they have always had difficulty controlling their weight, you may be able to subtly help them to do that without being too obvious about your effort. If you know they have a history of drug or alcohol abuse, you may want to avoid friendships with other couples who drink or abuse drugs. If they are allergic to aspirin, you'd naturally want to make sure that nobody in the household purchases a medicine that contains aspirin.

Remember, having all this information brings a heightened awareness level to your relationship.

■ EMPLOYMENT

What jobs did your partner have once they finished high school or college? How long were they employed at each position, and what were the reasons they left each job? Did they leave each job because they were fired, or did they leave voluntarily?

■ FINANCIAL MATTERS

Was the amount of money your partner earned as a young adult generally sufficient to meet their monthly needs? Were they able to stay within their budget? In retrospect, does your partner think that they were fairly disciplined when it came to the financial part of their young adult life? Did they go into debt? If so, what important lesson did they learn about financial responsibility from that experience?

■ ADULT YEARS

Many of the same topics discussed above in young adult years also apply to adult years. It is a good idea to encourage your partner to continue to be open and honest about their adult years, also.

■ MARRIAGE

If your partner was married previously, it will be helpful for you to know as much about that failed relationship and their feelings about it as possible.

How did they meet their former spouse? How old were they? Was your partner immediately attracted to that person? How long did they date before decided to get married? As the wedding day approached, did they think that they had made the right decision to marry this person? Was the marriage ever filled with love, respect, caring and friendship, or was it always lacking in some or many ways? Did your partner ever consider their former spouse to be their best friend? Did they share their deepest feelings and thoughts with one another? What was the strongest part of your partner's relationship with their former spouse? What was the biggest problem your partner had with their former spouse? What was the primary reason they decided to separate? Was the separation and divorce something your partner wanted, or was it something their former spouse wanted? What was the final decree of dissolution that was entered? If there were children involved, was your partner awarded joint custody or sole custody?

How did your partner adjust to the separation and divorce? Did they seek help from professionals or others in order to help get themselves through the emotional aspect of the process?

■ CHILDREN

Does your partner enjoy being a parent? Do they find it easy to be patient with their children? Do they think being a parent is what they expected, or is it different? Does your partner believe that they are a good parent? Do they think that they could be a better parent? What does your partner wish they had done differently with their children? Is their relationship with their children flourishing, or not too good? What was the scariest moment they has had as a parent? What is the hardest decision they have had to make as a parent?

■ A FINAL NOTE

If you share the "passkey to your past" with your partner, and they share their past with you, it will help you both to begin your relationship without any pretenses. It will help you both to disclose not only the good things about your character and life up to this point, but also those negative things of which we are all ashamed. It will leave you both with little — if anything — to hide from each other. This full disclosure will help you from the start to be open and honest with each other, so that telling the truth about *everything* — even the smallest detail — is comfortable in your relationship.

It will help you both to interpret the real meaning behind the things you say. It will help you and your partner to be sensitive to each other's areas of weaknesses in order to offer your strengths to help offset them. It will help you both to feel each other's moods by casually observing, not asking. It will help you to be sensitive to those things that make you both feel self-conscious, so they can avoid being the cause of any such feeling. It will help you be more aware of any physical or emotional change that may place your partner in danger. It will help you to avoid focusing on any of your partner's possible imperfections, and instead redirect your attention to their attributes.

And finally, by being aware of your partner's past feelings, experiences, and relationships, you are better able to learn to anticipate the needs of your partner so you can more adequately satisfy those needs.

PART THREE

Abandonment Comes In Many Forms

INTRODUCTION TO PART 3

HANDLE WITH CARE

*A*ll of us are fragile. We can easily feel hurt — especially by those people who we love and who we want to love us. We feel hurt if our partner breaks promises he or she made to us. We feel hurt if our partner's attitude or behavior falls short of our expectations, and our partner feels hurt if our expectations are so high that we seem impossible to please. We feel hurt if we're yelled at or if our partner continually interrupts while we're trying to express our feelings or talk about our day. We feel hurt if our partner doesn't share in the responsibility of taking care of the house or the children. We feel hurt if our partner says things that cause us to feel unworthy.

We can feel hurt for so many reasons that it's impossible to discuss them all here. However, it's important to remember that when we are hurt by someone we love, we tend to feel that they have begun to abandon us. Each time we are hurt, we add another brick to an invisible barrier we build to shield ourselves from being hurt again. The more times we are hurt, the more bricks are added to our defense, and the higher and thicker the barrier becomes. Finally, this barrier inhibits both our awareness and the expression of our feelings. When we don't express our feelings, a portion of our strength is diverted to blocking and repressing them. The process of living our lives becomes even more exhausting, and we don't perform as well as we should in our work, with our children, or with our own personal struggle to become a little better each day.

Sadly, when we don't express our negative feelings to our partner — and they therefore don't learn that we feel hurt — we also tend to stop openly expressing *positive* feelings of love and warmth to them. They naturally begin to resent the fact that they are only receiving a fraction of the love that they once were receiving. Because you haven't expressed your feelings of being hurt, your partner doesn't understand why you're not expressing loving feelings. In response, they begin to build a barrier of their own. They vent their frustration at not being loved in the way to which they had became accustomed by perpetuating behavior that causes you to feel even more abandoned. Eventually each partner feels totally abandoned by the other. Each feels unloved and unwanted, and the entire problem may have started somewhat innocently and unintentionally.

This part of the book identifies 28 behavior patterns that may cause either you or your partner to feel abandoned; to add a brick to your respective barriers. These behavior patterns have also been grouped into five categories: Abusive Behavior, Distancing Behavior, Avoidance Behavior, Chauvinistic Behavior, and Untrustworthy Behavior. There is no way to help you determine how high and thick that barrier must become for your relationship to be in serious jeopardy. Suffice to say, though — aside from hitting your partner with a solid right cross or having an affair — there may be no single or even multiple abandonment-causing behaviors that can be terminal to the relationship, *if* you can learn to recognize those behaviors and eliminate them from your and your partner's behavior patterns.

The objective of this chapter is to help you recognize what behaviors cause you or your partner to add bricks to your respective barriers. Hopefully, if you become familiar with the things that cause you and your partner to feel abandoned:

• you will try not to be the cause of any such feeling;

- you will recognize if you have been the cause of an abandonment causing feeling and you'll correct the mistake before another brick is added to your barrier;
- if you are the recipient of an abandonment-causing behavior, you will be able to gently express your feelings rather than subconsciously add another brick to your barrier; and
- you will be able to make your partner feel comfortable eliminating that behavior from their behavior pattern.

CHAPTER 8

ABUSIVE BEHAVIOR

■ SAYING THINGS THAT CAUSE
FEELINGS OF UNWORTHINESS

Imagine, just for a moment, that you're a child again. Perhaps you're only four or five years old. Your mom and dad are, of course, practically your entire world, and all you're really hoping is that they like you, love you, accept you, and support you. Imagine that from the time you're four or five years old until you leave their home, the only words you hear from your mom and dad are "You're really a good person... You're so conscientious... You're smart... I'm proud of you... You try so hard... I admire you... I respect you... Good try... I like you... I love you." As a matter of fact, your parents never say anything to you that would cause you to feel unworthy. Imagine what a good self-image you would have.

Now imagine that from the time you're four or five years old until you left their home, you continually heard your parents say things to you like "How could you do something so stupid?... You're a lazy good-for-nothing... You have your head up your ass... You're an ignoramus... You'll never succeed at anything you do... I don't like you; get out of my sight... You're obnoxious... I'm ashamed of you." All you ever wanted them to do is love you. If they didn't like you and think you were worthy, why should you feel good about yourself? If your parents didn't love you, who would? Of course, chances are that you *haven't* grown up feeling good about yourself and you struggle each day trying to overcome those feelings of unworthiness that were deeply imbedded in you by your parents.

For those of you who know what I'm talking about, you know how difficult it's been. Before moving on, though, let's make one thing clear. You are *not* unworthy. Your parent or parents who said those things to you were not well. They, too, were raised by parents who made them feel unworthy about themselves. They didn't intentionally hurt you. That doesn't excuse their behavior, but I'm telling you that so you understand that they probably know they've really screwed up and they are really sorry.

You need to forgive them and yourself for any of those terrible things in your life you've done that proved to yourself and your parents that they were right about you. You need to forgive yourself for letting those terrible things they said about you become a self-fulfilling prophecy. Forgive them and move on, doing the very best you can each day to become the person you truly were destined to become. Go ahead — beat yourself up emotionally for the next couple of days; be really angry at yourself for being such a jerk. But two mornings from now, when you awake in the morning, say these words: "I forgive myself for doing so many terrible things." Repeat those words to yourself daily before you get out of bed. Truly forgive yourself. It's time you should do this.

Now back to the subject at hand. If you were raised by parents who made you feel unworthy, you may have been saying terrible things to your partner — as well as to your children — that cause them to feel unworthy about themselves. If you have being doing this, stop it today. Never, never again say anything to your partner that causes them to feel even slightly unworthy. As a matter of fact, inundate them with positive statements. Each day, intentionally say things that are designed to help them to feel good. You'll be absolutely amazed at the immediate change in their attitude — especially if their barrier hasn't "topped out." (If it has, Chapter 15 — "Breaking Down Barriers" — will help you with an approach to dealing with this.)

If you have been saying things to your partner that have caused them to feel unworthy about themselves, you have certainly not been your partner's best friend. Additionally, you have pushed buttons that cause them to subconsciously recall all the negative things that were said to them by their parents. If that's true, the barrier that they have built that protects them from you is probably twice as high and twice as thick, because it needs to not only act as a defense against *you* but also against their parents, regardless of whether they are living or deceased.

If you have been the recipient of negative input from your partner, you need to sit down with them, hold their hands in yours, make sure there are no distractions, touch their chin slightly so that you move their head in your direction so their eyes are focused directly on your eyes, and say these words: "Honey, I really want to love you. I want us to love each other for the rest of our lives and I want us to be best friends. When I was a child my parents hurt me terribly by saying things to me that made me feel badly about myself. They called me stupid, lazy, and said in many different ways that I was not worthy. When you say things to me like (repeat the words they have used with you), you hurt me terribly. You not only remind me of how I felt when my parents said terrible things to me, you make me feel like you don't think I'm a worthy, good person, too. Please don't hurt me like that anymore."

Hopefully, your partner will respond appropriately. If they don't respond with gentleness and understanding, perhaps there isn't going to be too much you can do to reach them.

If you have been the cause of making your partner experience feelings of unworthiness, explain to your partner how badly you feel for what you have been doing, and make an undying commitment — both to your partner and yourself — never to say anything negative to your partner again. You must never again say any of the following words (or any others that are similar) to your partner again: You're stupid. You're lazy. You can't cook. You're fat. Why can't you wear your hair like your friend. She's so pretty. He's so handsome. You're a lousy lover.

■ SAYING THINGS THAT CAUSE EMBARRASSMENT

We all feel insecure about some personal things. Some of us believe that we are not as well educated or as smart as we'd like to be, or we think we're not as pretty or handsome as some of our friends, family members, or co-workers. We feel that we're too fat or too thin. Our hair — if we have hair left — is too fine, too gray, not cut in the proper way, or simply the wrong color. We wish we had a better job and earned more money. All of us wish we had more talent so we could sing, dance, paint, write, or sculpt. Most of us wish we were more athletic and in better physical shape. We all are still striving to achieve goals that, so far, have been just out of reach, and many of us wish our relationships with our partner, children, friends, and family members were better.

When we feel insecure we may also feel self-conscious and defensive about our feelings of inadequacy and of our personal desires and goals. Those feelings are private. They are not feelings casually shared with others. When two people commit to be partners and best friends, it is inherently understood that those private, very personal feelings you each learn about each other are never divulged to anyone else. The reason we are embarrassed is that there is some truth about us that is revealed before we're ready to accept it, and we wish to hide from it. In any relationship, it is inherently understood that a breach of that commitment not to reveal that truth — even something seemingly minor — would be a serious breach of trust.

One of the major complaints that Karen expressed about Bernie was that he frequently exposed her feelings of inadequacy to friends or family. One night when they were out for dinner with Bernie's boss and his wife, Karen ordered chocolate layered cake for her desert. Just as she finished ordering this desert Bernie said "Karen, why did you order cake, aren't you trying to lose some weight?" Bernie either wasn't thinking or didn't care that Karen would be embarrassed by his comment. Bernie however, exposed one of Karen's feelings of inadequacy which should never have been exposed in the privacy of their own bedroom, let alone in public. An "I'm sorry," "I just thought I was helping you" or "you're being too sensitive, no one thought anything about it" just doesn't work to make Karen's embarrassment dissipate.

Remember Karen and Bernie from the beginning of this book? As you might recall, Karen and Bernie had many more problems than simply Bernie's being insensitive to Karen's feelings of inadequacy. But if this had been an unusual circumstance instead of a regular occurrence, when Karen and Bernie arrived home that evening, Karen could have said to Bernie, "Bernie, sit down with me for a moment please." (When they sit down together Karen should be facing Bernie and holding his hands in hers. Her eye contact should be perfect and she should gently make sure his is good, too.) "Bernie, you hurt me tonight and I want to explain how you did this and why it hurt me. Please don't say anything until I'm finished. When you told me in front of your boss and his wife that I shouldn't order cake because I'm trying to lose weight, that really embarrassed me. I know I'm trying to lose weight and you know that, too. It's no one else's business. If I was screwing up, that's my problem and it didn't need to be called to my attention in front of them. Please don't do it again, it really hurt me."

Hopefully, Bernie would have understood Karen's gentle explanation and said, "I'm sorry, I won't do it again." If he had simply said those words, Karen would not have added another brick to her barrier — provided Bernie didn't ever embarrass her again like that. Remember, if he *does* do it again, Karen probably won't take the time to sit down with him again. She'll verbally chop his head off, and add two or more bricks to her barrier.

■ BEING CRITICAL

If you've ever either thought or said "nothing I do is good enough" to someone with whom you are in a relationship, you know what it feels like to be in a relationship with someone who is being critical. While we are all truly alone, a relationship should offer us the opportunity to be alone with another. In the best relationships, each of us is permitted to be completely natural and free to become our best, to fail, to grow, and to experiment. When we are in a relationship with someone who is being critical of us, we feel rejected — especially when the criticism is not based on a real shortcoming. We also feel self-conscious of those aspects of our life about which our partner is being critical.

For those of us who have been raised by a parent who was critical, we know how it feels to focus on our imperfections. We blamed our parents for a lack of encouragement and yet secretly felt as though we were not good enough. Some of us withdrew and felt unnecessarily pessimistic, while others of us are still trying to prove to others — and especially ourselves — that we are worthy. Some of us avoided dealing with our imperfections, stopped growing, and made the criticism a self-fulfilling prophecy. When we are in a relationship with someone who is critical, all the past as well as the current feelings of inadequacy are triggered by the partner who is being critical. The cycle of feeling rejected, feeling unworthy, and letting the criticism become a self-fulfilling prophecy continues.

While we are partners with someone who is being critical, and we remain embedded in this cycle, we are not free to forgive ourselves for our failures because we are continually being reminded of them. We are not free to become our best, to overcome our real shortcomings, and to begin to work on improving ourselves so that we can feel worthy of our own respect.

If you are being criticized by your partner, you may have expressed (or are expressing) your anger at this by being resentful and rebellious. You may find yourself unwilling to compromise on any issue without feeling that you have been cheated. You may also have a persistent feeling of being controlled. You may be feeling that your partner is also trying to change you, and that, once again, nothing you do feels like it's good enough.

And that doesn't feel good.

If you feel this way, you may have been manipulated, controlled, and criticized by one or both of your parents. Your critical nature with your partner is a perpetuation of the cycle started by your parents with you. There is an answer to this problem, though — which, in part at least, was created by your being so critical. Remember, in the best relationships each of us is permitted to be completely natural and free; to become our best, to fail, to grow, and to experiment. The answer is to let your partner be free — even if doing so permits them to reject you.

That's a scary thought, isn't it? You'll be running a big risk, especially after being so critical and controlling. Your partner could leave you, and it may very well happen. But if you don't let your partner be free, free to be themselves, they will reject you sooner or later anyway. It's only a matter of time. Your only chance to save your relationship is to let your partner be free to become their best or worst.

■ YELLING

When you yell at your partner, the effect will be the same as if you had whispered the same words so softly that they were unable to hear them. Your partner cannot hear your words if you shout them. They can see your mouth moving. They can see your eyes bulging and the veins in your neck protruding. They can even hear a loud noise originating from your vocal chords and coming out of your mouth, but they cannot understand what you are trying to say. They cannot hear your words because they hide behind that barrier they've built to protect themselves from you. The barrier that will shield them from the pain inflicted upon them by your yelling.

When you yell, your partner feels that you don't like them. They certainly don't feel that you love them. They feel that you don't care if your yelling causes them to be afraid of you. They think that you are trying to intimidate them rather than be their friend. They feel that you are breaking your promise never to hurt them. They feel abandoned. They feel defensive. Their probable response is to lash out at you, too. They will say things that are intended to inflict the same degree — or even a greater degree — of pain onto you as you are inflicting onto them. When your partner does this, you lash back, and the cycle continues. Another brick is added to both of your barriers.

If you are being yelled at by your partner, you must try to help them understand the effect their yelling has upon you. If you are the one doing the yelling, you must understand that yelling is an abandonment-causing behavior and that you must stop if you hope to have a healthy relationship with your partner.

Here's an example.

Of course, it's sad when any couple comes into my office to ask me to mediate the dissolution of their marriage. From time to time though, I hear things that are unusual and even pretty strange. One such time occurred when Eric, age 28, came into our office without his wife Meredith, age 26. He explained that they each wanted to have an individual meeting with me before they met with me together. I confirmed with Meredith that she was in agreement with this approach.

I asked Eric why he thought their marriage needed to be dissolved. You must remember that, as we noted in our introduction, the primary reasons we hear from men are "she doesn't trust me…she doesn't understand the pressure I'm under…she's always criticizing me…she only cares about herself…she's lazy." Eric, however, had something slightly different to say: "About one year ago, Meredith moved her boyfriend into our home. I put up with it for the last year, but it was really hard for me in the middle of the night." I asked Eric what he meant, although I was almost afraid to hear his answer. "Well, Andy has been sleeping in Meredith's room since he moved into our home. I can deal with it during the day but at night when I hear them doing their thing, and Meredith is making the same sounds she made when we had sex, I get really upset." I asked Eric what he did, and he told me "I yell at them to keep it down, but Meredith doesn't hear me or at least she says she doesn't."

Apart from the fact that this situation and Eric's tolerance of it is bizarre, the fact that Eric mentioned that Meredith doesn't hear him yelling is what struck me as interesting. So I asked Eric if, before Andy moved into his home, he yelled at Meredith often. He said he did. I asked him why he yelled at her and he answered that he needed to get his point across and he was afraid that she wouldn't listen to him unless he yelled. He said that his dad yelled at his mom all the time and that she didn't seem to mind. He said his parents had been married for 28 years before his mom died of a heart attack when she was 50 years old.

Eric yelled at Meredith for the 10 years they were married. She couldn't (or didn't want to) hear him then and she certainly couldn't hear him while she was having sex with Andy. As a matter of fact, Eric's yelling probably became music to her ears while she was with Andy.

■ COMPARING YOUR PARTNER TO ANOTHER MAN OR WOMAN

When you compare your partner to another person of the same sex, you convey the impression that

...you don't like them as they are,

...you wish they were like someone else,

...you are insensitive to their feeling hurt by the comparisons,

...they may have reason to feel unworthy,

...they shouldn't feel secure about your feelings for them, and

...they may not be able to trust you.

I understand that I am making a simple, possibly light, comparison sound devastating. I believe that when you even jokingly or innocently compare your partner to another person of the same sex, the short-term — as well as the long-term — effect on your relationship can be devastating.

The following are examples of how many of us, perhaps innocently, compare our partner to someone else, and how our partner feels when this happens.

She says: "My friend Harriet and her husband bought the most beautiful new home. I wish we could live in a home like that."

He feels: "She wishes I earned more money; that I was smarter. She wishes she were married to someone else who could provide her with a new home. If she finds someone who makes her feel loved and makes more money, she would leave me. My best isn't, or hasn't been, good enough."

We can hear many of you saying, "Come on now, what's wrong with saying that I wish we could live in a larger, more beautiful home? We all wish we could have more, newer, better, or larger of everything." That's true, but men are big-time sensitive to the issue of whether or not they are good providers. If you verbalize your wish, he perceives it as a comparison. His mind goes crazy with all kinds of thoughts that are perhaps not even remotely connected to your statement. You need to be careful of his possible insecurity about needing to be your "hero" and providing you with everything you've ever dreamt of having. He may perceive any verbalized wish you make as a comparison to all other men. His response may be one of becoming more withdrawn; he may respond by putting you down. He may make a sarcastic remark.

Any negative response he makes to your comment will seem to you like an overreaction to an innocent remark. You may even feel angry that he perceived your statement as degrading, and say something that will make him feel even more defensive. Be careful now. Understand that his ego is very fragile. He *knows* you wish for more. He wishes for more for you, too. He strives to be not only your hero, but his own hero too.

He looks back at a woman who passes as you and he are walking together.

She feels: "What does she have that I don't have? Why does he have to do that?"

She pretends she doesn't care. She pretends it's cute. She may even say something like "Did you see that?" But the truth is, men — *don't do it*. If you really want to be her best friend, don't even take the chance that it might hurt her even a little. "Did you see that?" Your response should be "What, honey?" and distract her attention by pointing out something else. She'll know you saw that woman, and possibly found her attractive. But she'll also know that you didn't want to hurt her even a little. She'll love that you are perceptive and protective of her feelings.

He gawks at some young thing in the *Playboy* centerfold.

She feels: "I'm unattractive by comparison; overweight; out of shape. I'm not as young as I'd like to be and I'm unappreciated. I'm angry that he'd even be looking at a nude picture of another woman in front of me. If some young, pretty thing made a play for him, he'd have an affair. He's not satisfied with me. I have to try harder to be attractive and sexy; I should try to please him more in bed."

Paul and Sandy are still married, but Paul doesn't keep his 100-plus *Playboy* magazine collection hidden underneath his bed. As a matter of fact, it's our guess that he doesn't keep them at all any more.

Paul couldn't understand why Sandy stopped making love to him about the time he began receiving his subscription of *Playboy* at their home. She never told him the reason. She only stopped. When they came into my office, I asked Sandy why she had filed for divorce. She said that Paul was always looking at and probably thinking about other women all the time. Paul seemed incredulous at the suggestion.

He said, "That's not true. I think you're beautiful. I never look at or even think about other women." Sandy shot back, "Oh yeah? What about the *Playboy* magazines you keep under our bed? I'm sure the pages are sticky, too, because until you get rid of those disgusting magazines I'm not going to begin to think about having sex with you."

It was the first time that Sandy had told Paul that when they were in bed, all she could think about was the fact that he loved looking at pictures of young, beautiful women, who for sure hadn't had a baby yet. Sandy and Paul had three children. I recommended a competent marriage counselor who was able to help them deal with this issue and other issues that had caused them both to feel abandoned.

■ COMMITTING ANY ACT OF UNWANTED PHYSICAL TOUCHING

You should expect to be treated with respect. You have the right to express your own feelings. You have the right to say "no" without feeling guilty. You have the right to be listened to when you say "no" and to be taken seriously.

Yes, *you* may be a battered person if…
…you are frightened of your partner's temper.
…you are often compliant because you are afraid to hurt your partner's feelings or are afraid of your partner's anger.
…you often apologize for your partner's behavior when you are treated badly.
…you have been hit, kicked, shoved, or had things thrown at you by your partner when they were jealous or angry.
…you make decisions about activities and friends according to what your partner wants or how your partner reacts.

Yes, *your partner* may be a batterer if…
…they are very jealous and attempt to know your whereabouts all the time.
…they sulk silently when upset.
…they have an explosive temper.
…they criticize and put you down a lot.

...they believe that it is their role to be in charge, or have contempt for the opposite sex.

...they control your behavior, money, and decisions.

...they have broken things, thrown things at you, hit, shoved, slapped, choked, punched, or kicked you when they were angry.

...they were physically or emotionally abused by a parent.

...they expect you to follow their orders or advice.

...they experience extreme highs and lows; they are extremely kind one time and extremely cruel another time.

...they talk about using guns, knives, or other lethal weapons to "get even."

...they are cruel to animals and abusive to children.

...they over-react to little problems and frustrations.

...they force you to have hurtful sex or are hurtful during sex.

If your partner is hitting you, treating you roughly, or physically forcing you to do what you don't want to do, do not think that this person will change for the better. Your partner doesn't come close to having an idea of what it means to be your best friend. You are already a battered person and should seek help now. Without some kind of help, the violence will usually get worse. Remember, the end result can be death.

CHAPTER 9

DISTANCING BEHAVIOR

■ SMOKING

Ladies, how many times have you been near a man and thought to yourself, "He smells so good!"? He may not even have been wearing cologne. It may just have been the fragrance naturally emanating from his body. And men, how often have you been ever so close to a woman who smells so sweet that you just want to snuggle into her neck and stay there the rest of the day and night? Their cleanliness invites closeness.

By the same token, when you are near someone who smokes cigarettes, their entire body — including their hair — smells of cigarette smoke. It doesn't smell good; it's vile. Kissing them is not a pleasant experience, no matter how attractive they may be. The odor makes most of us sick to our stomach.

People who smoke are, of their own volition, choosing to shorten the term of their life. By the nature of the fact that they smoke, they are conveying the message to others that their self-image is so poor, they don't care if they live or die. They also portray the image of a person who is so irresponsible that they, while smoking, endanger the life of others who are in their presence as a result of the debilitating effect of second-hand smoke. They may verbally ask you to come close, and to be close to them, but through their behavior they are conveying the opposite message.

If you are currently a smoker, you are evidencing distancing behavior that not only causes your partner to add another brick to their barrier each time you smoke another cigarette, but also you are killing yourself and any love which might be left between you and your partner, especially if your partner is a non-smoker. It might be a good idea to stop smoking now if you value not only your life, but also the life of your partner, other family members and the life of your relationship.

■ ABUSING DRUGS OR ALCOHOL

Why does someone abuse drugs or alcohol? Each person individually has their own specific conscious or subconscious reasons, but in general it is because they choose to obliterate their mind so that, for the time they are high, they don't have to deal with life's daily problems.

Even if you drink or get high with your partner and once in a while feel that being high heightens your awareness and sensitivity, it is not true. That feeling is artificially stimulated and isn't based upon *truly* being in touch. If you are getting high and drinking by yourself, while you're high, you and your partner are in two different worlds.

Your partner feels as though you have truly abandoned them. They are disgusted by your behavior, even if they once in a while pretend that they're not. As a matter of fact, the drug or alcohol is, by and of itself, the barrier that prevents intuitive interaction between you and your partner. Unlike all other distancing behavior — which results in another brick being added to a barrier — drug or alcohol abuse is simultaneously both the *cause* of the barrier and the barrier itself.

If your partner is abusing drugs or alcohol, you should seek the help of Alcoholics Anonymous, and encourage your partner to seek counseling also.

■ BEING OVERLY ATTENTIVE
TO SOMEONE OF THE OPPOSITE SEX

Regardless of how secure we may feel in a relationship, we all sometimes feel insecure. When we are not feeling especially confident or good about ourselves, we may tend to feel anxious if our partner pays too much attention to someone of the opposite sex. If you wish to be your partner's best friend, you need to be able to determine when they are feeling somewhat insecure about themselves, and be careful not give them additional anxiety by giving them reason to be concerned about your loyalty, faithfulness, and attraction to them.

Don't misunderstand what I'm trying to say — I'm not talking about a friendly hello, a warm smile, or a firm handshake with someone of the opposite sex. I'm talking about being flirtatious, laughing a little too much, or touching another person — in the hope that you'll elicit a positive response from that other person.

It's difficult to tell someone not to feel insecure. A person either feels secure or doesn't feel secure, and generally the feeling of security will come from a combination of how a person feels about themselves and how they feel about the relationship they're in. If a couple are really best friends and all parts of the relationship are healthy, it isn't too often that either partner will feel insecure about the other's loyalty to them and to the relationship. But even so, you want to be careful not to do anything that induces anxiety, because this is your *best friend*; this is the person to whom you are devoted. And if you are the cause, even innocently, of some level of anxiety, you are not being your partner's best friend. So, when you are in the presence of someone of the opposite sex, you want to be conscious not to be flirtatious, and not to do anything that makes your partner feel that you are looking for more than innocent, normal attention from that other person.

If you are not careful on a consistent basis, and your partner feels insecure about your loyalty and about the relationship, the effect will be that your partner will eventually increase the size of their barrier by adding brick upon brick — and that barrier will be a difficult one to break down. Furthermore, your partner may retaliate by being flirtatious with someone else, too.

Every part of your relationship should be comfortable. It should be comfortable when you are together. It should be comfortable when you are alone. It should be comfortable when you are in the presence of other people. In order for you to visualize this level of comfort, hold your hands up in front of you so your palms are facing each other and your fingers are apart. Now slowly move your hands closer together until they are just about to touch each other. Let your fingers from each hand move slowly in between the fingers of the other hand, and let them fall comfortably and relaxed together, resting ever so gently and completely relaxed against each other. *That's* the feeling you should have when you are with your best friend. Totally comfortable, peaceful, and relaxed.

If you tend to pay too much attention to a member of the opposite sex — perhaps the husband or wife of a couple with whom you're friends, or someone with whom you work — the anxiety your partner may feel creates a tension between the two of you that undermines the totally comfortable, peaceful, and relaxed feeling that you want to achieve.

We are afraid that we may lose the relationship. We are afraid to find out that the love we think our partner feels for us is not as great as what we imagined it to be. We are afraid that our partner will find someone else more appealing, attractive, and sexy than they find us. We are afraid to face the realization that we are not as attractive as we were when we first met our partner. We are afraid of all the ramifications if our partner falls in love with someone else.

The fear we experience when our partner pays too much attention to someone of the opposite sex may very well cause us to react in an angry way. It would take a *very* secure person in an *extremely* healthy relationship to say to his or her partner, "Gosh, it looked to me like you were paying an awful lot of attention to 'this person,' and it made me feel afraid of losing you and afraid of your attraction to this person. I wish you wouldn't do that."

Most of us are not that secure. When most of us are afraid, our reaction will be an angry and hostile one that is the direct impetus to creating an argument — which causes your partner to add to their defense and put another brick in their barrier.

So here again, we may have a couple in a really good relationship, where one of the partners, for whatever reason, for whatever they are experiencing at the moment, looks to be (and perhaps *is*) having a "moment" with someone of the opposite sex, perhaps in the presence of their partner. The fearful reaction of the partner is negative, which creates a similar reaction from the initiating partner, and the relationship falls out of balance for a moment or two — or maybe even longer.

It's really important to remember that if you are the person who acted angrily at your partner for paying too much attention to someone of the opposite sex, and you — after reflection on their behavior and their response — decide that you over-reacted, you have to *very quickly* tell your partner that you are sorry, that you blew it, that you should have handled this situation much differently than the way you dealt with it. Tell your partner that you were feeling really anxious, rather insecure, and rather badly about yourself. Explain how you feel. If you don't do this very quickly, there will be tension. And tension means more bricks are added to your partner's barrier.

If you are the one who was accused of paying too much attention to a person of the opposite sex, you must maintain an awareness of how your partner may be feeling about your too personal contact with someone else. You must be careful not to be too flirtatious again.

■ SPENDING TOO MUCH TIME WITH YOUR FRIENDS

In an ideal situation, you and your partner are such good friends that you want to spend most of your spare time with each other. Of course, in reality — except in very rare cases — that's the exception rather than the rule. On the other hand, our days are so busy — working and taking care of all our responsibilities — that it is difficult to spend a lot of time with a friend or a group of friends other than your partner and still be sure that you and your partner are spending enough time together.

What is enough time together? "Enough time together" means the amount of time necessary for neither of you to feel that the other wants to be with someone else. Consciously scheduling time is not necessarily a good idea; it can leave the relationship lacking in spontaneity. Try, however, to "outline" your week — perhaps mentally, if not on paper — and plan ahead. Say "Let's go to the club on Tuesday to work out," or "Let's plan on going to dinner Wednesday night," or "Let's plan on being alone on Saturday evening." Although it's not a definite "date," which eliminates many of the possibilities of spontaneity, it's a planned time for the two of you to be together.

In terms of distancing behavior, however, it is necessary to touch on what your partner feels if you are spending more time with a friend — a same sex friend rather than opposite sex friend, of course. The message you convey to your partner is that you don't enjoy being with them. If your partner complains that "We don't spend any time together," what they are really saying to you is "I need to feel that you want to be with me"… "I need to feel that you don't want to be with someone else"… "I need to have you with me more than what we have been, so that we can feel connected."

If you reject that plea, your partner begins to become defensive and — you guessed it — adds another brick to that barrier of theirs. And on each subsequent occasion that you spend more time with your friend than your partner — even though your partner may not be saying something specific to you about it — they add still another brick to their barrier as they build up further resentment toward you because you are not choosing them as your primary playmate.

Is this jealousy or insecurity? Well, not in the same context as when one of the partners is attracted to someone of the opposite sex. It's more of a feeling of wanting to be with your partner in other ways than just going through the daily tumult of living life together. Here you are, living in the same home, worrying about paying your bills, worrying about raising your children to be healthy and happy people, struggling to stay healthy yourselves, and dealing with all the things you need to deal with each day. There needs to be some break from just dealing with these issues and enjoy fun time simply being by yourselves together. If your partner is taking that very valuable — and very little — time that you have for each other and spending it with a friend rather than you, it's not abnormal to feel angry or resentful.

Such was the case with Rick and Stephanie. Rick is a real estate developer specializing in apartment properties. Stephanie is a CPA with a major accounting firm. They have a combined income of more than $100,000 a year. They own a beautiful 3,000-square-foot home. They have one 6-year-old child and they have lots of friends. Rick's friends consist of those with whom he grew up, because Rick and Stephanie live in the same city Rick has lived in all his life. Stephanie's friends, on the other hand, are those she's met since she's been living in Rick's hometown (where she attended college) and those she's met at work — although she is close with some of the wives of the couples Rick and Stephanie socialize with on weekends.

Their weekly schedule goes something like this. Rick gets up at about 4:30 each weekday morning. He reads the paper, jogs three miles, showers and shaves, and dresses to leave for work. Stephanie gets up at about 6 a.m. She wakes up their son, Ricky, and prepares breakfast for him. By this time, Rick is ready to leave for work. He kisses Ricky and Stephanie good-bye, tells them both he'll be home before dinner — at about 7 p.m. — and, before he's out the door, begins speaking on his cellphone to the general contractor who is working on his current project.

Stephanie makes sure Ricky is dressed before she jumps into the shower. She spends about 45 minutes getting ready for work. When finished, she throws a load of wash into the machine and writes a note for their maid, asking her to put the clothes in the washing machine into the dryer and to make dinner for Ricky. She explains that she and Rick won't be home until about 7 p.m. This evening Rick gets home about 6:45 p.m. — just in time to get a call from Stephanie, telling him that she won't be home until about 9 p.m. She explains that she and the project coordinator on the audit she's working on need to meet with their client. This evening they're going to take him out to dinner. She asks to speak with Ricky, says she's sorry but Mommy has to work late, and asks Rick to call their gardener because the sprinklers are not coming on at the times they should be. Stephanie arrives home at 9:30 p.m., as she does at least once or twice each week.

One other time during each week, Stephanie goes out with her girlfriends after work, and she spends one evening each week taking a two-hour accounting course.

Rick plays basketball once a week and also works out at the health club twice a week after work. He works out with Jonathan, a friend he's known since grammar school.

On Friday and Saturday nights Rick and Stephanie go out with their friends. Except for birthdays or their anniversary, they are rarely alone. Sunday mornings, Stephanie goes to church with Ricky. Rick plays golf with his college buddies, but he's generally home by 2 p.m.

Rick says that Stephanie's career is more important to her than he is. Stephanie says that Rick would rather play golf on Sunday with his buddies than being with her. Stephanie says that becoming a partner in her accounting firm is as important to her and the financial stability of their family as Rick's owning his own development company and building apartment buildings is to him. Rick can't understand why he shouldn't be able to play golf on his only day off with guys he's hung out with since childhood. Each feels abandoned by the other. Both have built barriers to protect themselves from the pain of feeling that their partner prefers to be with other people rather than to be with them.

Who's right? Is either right? Does it matter who's right? The answer is that it doesn't *matter* who is "right" when it comes to being your partner's best friend. Here's the concept to which you both must adhere if you are going to go through life together as best friends:

Your partner's perspective is your partner's perspective. It doesn't matter if it's right or wrong. It's your partner's perspective. Does that mean that you always have to give up your perspective if your perspective differs from that of your partner? No. It means that you both have to move slightly more toward middle ground so that both of you can feel peaceful. It means that you both must understand that it's you and your partner against the world. The two of you must come to a peaceful place with everything in your lives.

If you and your partner do not appreciate each other's perspective, everything becomes more difficult. It's more difficult to perform up to your highest standards at work. It's more difficult to maintain healthy family relationships. It's more difficult to raise your children to be healthy, happy human beings. It's more difficult for you to remain centered and to grow to become the person you were destined to become. It's more difficult to laugh with or to want to be sensuous with your partner. Very little feels as though it's in balance. Very little between the two of you flows naturally. Much of your interaction with one another seems contrived.

From Rick's point of view, does it really matter if he plays golf with his buddies every Sunday morning? Shouldn't he understand how wonderful Stephanie would feel being able to walk into church every *other* Sunday morning with him by her side? From Stephanie's perspective, does she have to go out with her girlfriends every week — especially if she's had to work the one or two nights that she has become accustomed to working? Shouldn't she understand how Rick would feel just being able to have her home that one extra night or two each week?

You cannot have a best friend forever if you are not willing to appreciate and understand your partner's perspective. You may go through the motions of being best friends, but you are not going to be in absolute rhythm with your partner. You are not going to be at absolute peace with your partner. Move more toward the middle on every issue. You'll be amazed at how much easier everything becomes and how you begin to prosper in every aspect of your life.

■ SIDING WITH SOMEONE ELSE
AGAINST YOUR PARTNER

As much as anything you can do, the distancing behavior of siding with someone else against your partner is one of the most severe forms of abandonment. It's simple: you're openly saying that you're not on your partner's side any more. To be your partner's best friend forever, you have to be a couple — teamed together in one common bond that always is bound by loyalty. There cannot be any reason for taking anyone else's side against your partner. This is especially true if you take either your mother's or father's side against your partner.

I think that siding with someone else against your partner is such a severe level of abandonment that I put it on the same level on the scale as having an affair. You cheat by siding with someone else against your best friend and it only has to happen once for it to be devastating to your relationship.

What does your partner feel when you side with someone else against them? They feel abandoned. They feel that you breached the covenant of loyalty. They feel that you are not being their friend. They feel that the promise you made when you took the oath of marriage has been broken. They feel that they can't trust you to be on their side all of the time. If you have sided with your mom and dad, or brother and sister, they feel that it is all of you against them. They feel hurt. They feel angry. They feel that they want to retaliate — and they *will* retaliate.

Emily and Jamie retained my services at first to mediate an issue concerning some civil litigation. Jamie is a high school psychologist and Emily is a teacher at a local school for the deaf. While they were in my office Emily picked up a copy of my *Man's Guide to Being a Woman's Best Friend* and began to look through it. She didn't say anything other than, "May I keep a copy of this book?" I naturally said "Yes." About one month later, Jamie called me and asked if he and Emily could set up an appointment. He explained that they were having problems in their relationship and were thinking about divorce.

Emily and Jamie have one child together: Carrie, who is 7 years old. Michele, Jamie's daughter from a previous marriage, is 15 years old and came to live with Emily and Jamie two years ago when Michele and her mother were not getting along. Jamie explained that he felt guilty about leaving the then four-year-old Michele when he and her mom divorced. He was determined to make up for all those years he had not been with Michele. Emily said that when the topic of Michele coming to live with them came up, she agreed to it, but privately resented the fact that Jamie wanted Michele to live with him, when he had previously said he was comfortable with Michele living with her mom (who had remarried).

Michele wanted as much of Jamie's undivided attention as possible. Jamie wanted to make amends to Michele, and he couldn't understand how Emily didn't appreciate all of the reasons Jamie wanted Michele to live with them. Michele's mom wouldn't stipulate to terminating the child support payment without the court ordering her to do so. Further, she felt that Jamie was intentionally trying to eliminate Michele from her life.

Does this situation create some feeling of anxiety in you as you read about Emily and Jamie? Imagine this, too: Michele senses Emily's resentment. She complains that everything she does is wrong when it comes to Emily. Jamie asks Emily, "Can't you please try to get along with Michele? We have to make this work." Michele cuddles with Jamie when he comes home from work. Emily feels as though she's not getting enough attention from Jamie, and occasionally even thinks "He never holds me like that."

As tension builds between Emily and Michele, Jamie begins to share with his daughter how he really feels about Emily's resentment about her coming to live with them. Michele and Jamie daily share private conversations about Emily's attitude, and Emily knows this. Emily feels abandoned by Jamie, and the resentment about Michele living with them increases. Emily eventually says to Michele, "It's easy to understand why you weren't getting along with your mom and stepdad. How could *anyone* live with you?"

How *could* Emily and Jamie have handled this situation? When it became apparent to Jamie that he had few alternatives other than to ask Emily if Michele can live with them, he could have said to Emily, "I'd like to discuss Michele coming to live with us. I know I promised that I wouldn't ask you this, but the circumstances have changed and I feel as though I need to be Michele's full-time dad now. I know it's going to be a difficult adjustment, but could we talk about it?"

Jamie must be willing to promise that he will not allow Michele to come between them, and at all costs he must keep that promise — even at the risk of alienating Michele. He must realize that almost every child coming into a situation like this will, consciously or subconsciously, attempt to pull their parent to them and away from their parent's spouse. Jamie must not have private conversations with Michele about Emily. He must never side with Michele against Emily. He must make it eminently clear to Michele that he loves her dearly, but he and Emily are not going to be divided on any issue. He must also make it clear to Michele that if she has a problem with Emily, she and Emily must work it out themselves, and that he will not allow himself to be placed in the middle under any circumstances. He must be Michele's dad, not her best friend. He must realize that he has only one best friend, and that is Emily.

The circumstances surrounding Emily and Jamie's relationship are not too unusual. They comprise another of those difficult situations many of us are facing in our daily lives.

Yes, you might feel that there is some rationale to siding with someone else against your partner. Yes, it may be difficult to take your partner's side against, for example, your mom or dad. But no matter *what* your rationale, when you chose to be your partner's mate — "until death do you part" — being best friends means that you don't side with anyone else against your partner about *anything*, regardless of the circumstances. If you have a difference of opinion with your partner, you talk to your partner about that difference. You don't let the rest of the world know that you may disagree with your partner. You don't abandon your partner in favor of taking someone else's side.

If you *do* side with someone else against your partner, you've alienated your partner — and the barrier this creates may become so high and thick that it is impenetrable. How do you correct this problem? (And there's no mistaking it: this is a *huge* problem because on the one hand you don't want to let your parents think that you are not devoted to them or that you don't love them, and on the other hand you don't want to let your partner think that you are going to continue to side with your parents.)

There is only one answer. You have to choose your partner's side if you want to stay together with your partner.

If this explanation makes sense to you but you don't know how to unwind the problem that's been created by siding with someone else, sit down with your partner, read them this section of the book, and tell them how very sorry you are for hurting them. If you sense that "I'm sorry" isn't good enough after you've evidenced a difference in your behavior, encourage your partner to go to a counselor with you.

■ INTERRUPTING

We have all had the experience of being with someone who continually talks about themselves and things in their life. We all want to be able to share parts of our life with others. It's natural to want to talk about ourselves. If you are often with a person who dominates the conversation and interrupts you when you are trying to share your thoughts, you undoubtedly will begin to be frustrated just by being with them, and may eventually decide that it's not worth remaining their friend.

When this person is not your partner, you can simply choose not to be with them as often or you can even choose to terminate the relationship. But if this person *is* your partner, you may feel trapped in the relationship and frustrated all the time. It's this lack of comfort in being with your partner that is the focus of this distancing behavior.

To be best friends with your partner, when you are together you both have to be completely peaceful. Your partner must know that you are not going to interrupt when they are talking to you. Your partner must not feel like they have to hurry to say something or be afraid that they are going to be interrupted. Your partner must not feel that you are going to disagree with them or change the subject before they finish talking. They must know that, whether it's something you want to listen to or not, they are going to be able to say what they want to say completely.

When your partner is being critical of something you've done, or commenting on your approach to a given situation, they must feel that you will listen and not interrupt and not be defensive about it. Your partner must be able to trust you to listen in order for there to be peacefulness in the relationship. It's this peaceful feeling that enables your partner to be open and communicative, rather than closed and afraid to express their feelings.

■ MAKING REPEATED ATTEMPTS AT CHANGING YOUR PARTNER

If you're not satisfied with your partner's behavior — or the way they look, or talk, or dress, or the job that they hold — and try to change them, your partner feels as though you don't like them. They feel on edge all the time while trying not to do things that displease you, or trying to do things that satisfy you. They are not comfortable feeling this way, and they are not peaceful when they are in your presence.

When you try to change your partner, they feel controlled by you. They feel that nothing they do is good enough for you. Every time they have this feeling, they add another brick to their barrier that separates the two of you. Eventually that barrier is so high that the separation between you is complete. They then *stop* trying to please you, and since nothing they do is good enough for you, the relationship comes to an end.

Remember, if you are the partner being critical, you must either accept your partner just the way they are and reinforce the positive things about them, or let them out of the relation-ship. If you are the partner being criticized, you must try to explain to your partner how their attempts at changing you makes you feel. Sure, that's a difficult thing to do. Perhaps you can encourage them to read this book so they will begin to understand how abandonment-causing behavior like this can be fatal to a relationship.

■ BEING INCONSIDERATE

Being considerate of your partner is making sure you take care of your responsibilities so your partner doesn't have to bear the burden of taking care of your responsibilities, too; anticipating your partner's needs by maintaining a heightened awareness; and reflecting upon your partner's responsibilities, schedule, and thought processes so you can do things for them that will make their days easier.

If your response is "yes" to even *some* of the following questions, you are being inconsiderate of your partner.

- Do you leave your dirty clothes on the floor?
- Do you leave the bathroom sink and surrounding area a mess after you use it?
- Do you finish the roll of toilet tissue and not replace it with a new roll?
- Do you leave dirty dishes in the sink?
- Do you fail to call when you are going to be later than your partner expects?
- Do you make noise while your partner is trying to sleep?
- Do you interrupt your partner when they are on the telephone?
- Do you leave your partner with an empty tank of gas in the car?
- Do you leave the dinner table without helping to remove the dishes?
- Do you throw your towel in the dirty clothes basket after only using it once?

- Do you let your partner be responsible for driving the kids around, even when they are exhausted?
- Do you let your partner go to the grocery store when you run out of milk?
- Do you fail to help your partner bring in the groceries after a major shopping trip?
- Do you dominate the conversation with stories about your work?
- Do you stay in the shower too long, using all the hot water?
- Do you walk too fast, leaving your partner to trail behind you?
- Do you make a risky left-hand turn into oncoming traffic with your partner next to you?
- Do you fail to be responsible about your personal hygiene?
- Do you use too much of your monthly income on your personal hobbies?
- Do you too often let your partner be the "bad guy" when disciplining your children?
- Do you fail to schedule your time properly, often making you and your partner late for engagements?
- Do you often show up late when you plan to meet your partner outside of the house?
- Do you use your partner's toothbrush?
- Do you fail to give your partner telephone messages?
- Do you fail to leave a note for your partner when you leave the house and they're not home?
- Do you respond negatively if your partner asks for your opinion about their appearance?
- Do you point out the existence of a pimple or blemish?
- Do you comment negatively about a new hairstyle?
- Do you pass gas in front of your partner?
- Do you read the newspaper while you and your partner are having a meal together?

- Do you take business or personal phone calls during dinner?

Most of these things that we've labeled as inconsiderate behavior are things that you should be doing as common courtesy for your partner. If you are guilty of a few of them most or all the time, your partner may be slightly annoyed, but it should not be considered as abandonment-causing behavior that would lead to your partner adding a brick to their barrier.

If, however, you've answered "yes" to many of these things, when considered together this may constitute an abandonment-causing behavior — and you'd better believe it's making your partner add to their barrier.

Correcting the problem of being inconsiderate is simple: Raise your awareness level and don't be lazy. Your partner will notice the difference and most likely will comment positively about the change.

■ BEING ON-LINE TOO MUCH

If they are going to feel that you truly are their best friend, your partner needs to know that your priority is spending time interacting with them, rather than doing something by yourself, like watching television, "surfing the Web," or being with friends. This doesn't mean to say that you must spend every spare minute with your partner, but if you become involved in too many activities without your partner being involved too, then you are perpetrating an abandonment-causing behavior.

For example, being on-line can be addicting. It is something you generally do by yourself, and it's easy to become fully engrossed being on the Internet, being in chat rooms, doing research, or writing e-mails to your friends or family. If you go on-line at, say, 7:30 or 8 at night, it's not unlikely that you might still be on-line late into the night, well after your partner has gone to bed. Since going to bed at night at the same time together — at least *most* of the time — is something that couples who are best friends should try to do, your late-night, on-line activities may make your partner feel abandoned as they lay in bed at night alone.

Going to bed at the same time together is a time to lay next to each other; a time to settle down and talk a little about something that happened during the day or even a time that you may lay next to each other watching TV, with your legs or feet touching those of your partner.

If your partner has gone to bed alone, they miss the wonderful feeling we get when we go to bed together. In addition to missing that wonderful feeling, they may also be missing being able to make love to you.

When you're on-line too much, or when you watch TV too much by yourself, and you don't go to bed together because of those activities, it constitutes a distancing behavior, which results in a feeling of abandonment for your partner. If it happens often and over a long period of time, your partner will unquestionably be adding bricks to their barrier. They don't add bricks every time it happens, but they may add a brick once a week or so. But the consistency of adding that brick once a week keeps that barrier growing — not only in height, but in thickness — and prevents you from being close, loving, best friends forever.

CHAPTER 10

AVOIDANCE BEHAVIOR

■ FAILING TO SHOW AFFECTION

There are two aspects of failing to show enough affection to your partner that need to be addressed. First, all of us need to be held, hugged, and kissed. We need to feel our body close to another. When your partner doesn't show you affection, you miss an integral part of a loving, warm relationship. And as a result of missing that, you become angry and resentful of their failure to keep the promise once made that they would always show affection to you. When you dated, there was probably lots of lovin' going on. There was kissing, and hugging, and making love, and it was terrific.

Second, if we are not held, hugged, and kissed by our partner, we begin to feel that our partner doesn't find us attractive or sexy any longer. We begin to try harder to be attractive and sensuous for our partner. We begin to be more sensitive to our partner's smile or innocent conversation with someone of the opposite sex. We begin to feel insecure about our partner's loyalty and devotion.

If affection stops during a relationship, the one not receiving the affection is going to feel as though the other is distancing themselves from that relationship. The person not receiving the affection is going to feel rejected. They begin to feel more and more rejected because their partner is avoiding being close to them, and they will add bricks to that barrier of theirs. When the offending partner finally reaches out to be affectionate, the other partner's wall blocks their response — and then *they* feel that they are being avoided. They, too, add bricks to *their* barrier, a vicious cycle begins, and the two continue to distance themselves from each other.

There isn't one abandonment-causing behavior that is more detrimental to your relationship than another. You may be more conscious of your partner's failing to show affection, however. This may be true if your father or mother failed to show you affection and you grew up not feeling worthy of being held, kissed, or caressed. When your partner doesn't show you affection, it brings back the feeling of loss you felt when you were a child. Any anger you felt toward your parent for not showing you affection begins to transfer to your partner. Your anger as a result of your partner not showing you affection can be combined with the anger you felt as a result of your *parent* not showing you affection.

■ FAILING TO ACCEPT AFFECTION

Failing to *accept* affection is as much an abandonment-causing behavior as failing to *give* affection. By not accepting your partner's affection, you clearly send your partner a message that you are rejecting them. For example, if your partner comes over to you and wants to snuggle with you, hold you, kiss you on your neck, kiss your ear, kiss your lips, and hold you and love you, and you say "Please, not now," or "Don't do that, I don't feel like it now," that is surely a way to reject your partner. What you're really saying is that "I don't want you to hold me," "I don't want you to kiss me," "I don't want to take the time to be with you." If you do this, your partner must be thinking, "What *is* the right time?" And since the answer to that question is "Every time is the right time," they must also think, "My partner must not feel good about being with me."

Here you are in this relationship. At some point in the early stages of the relationship — and perhaps many years into the relationship — your partner accepted your affection readily. But now you make advances to them in order to be loving, gentle, caring, warm, and sexy, and they say "not now," using whatever excuse they choose to use. In essence they hold up their hands in front of them as if they are school crossing guards and say "Stop! Don't come any closer... Don't invade my space." Talk about adding bricks: if this happens on a consistent basis, you add as many as you can lift onto that barrier so that your partner can't hurt you again. Failing to accept affection is as hurtful a thing to do to your partner as any other. It is even a more obvious abandonment-causing behavior than failing to *give* affection.

The interesting thing is that when you reject your partner's affection, there are a million excuses you may use, including "I have a headache," "I'm busy," "I have things to do," "Your breath smells," — and you may try to make them sound like they are meaningful. However, regardless of the excuse you use, none of them make any sense to your partner. Does saying "I'm busy" mean that you can't take even 10 seconds to accept love? Your partner thinks, "If you can't take 10 seconds to accept my love, I can't share *any* part of me with you," and another brick — or 10 bricks — is added to that barrier. You've hurt your partner when you don't accept their affection. The pain of their hurt will not go away until you reverse this trend.

■ FAILING TO BE OPEN ABOUT FEELINGS

Let's examine some of the reasons why you may not be open about sharing ("communicating") your feelings and the reason a lack of sharing may be causing you or your partner to feel abandoned.

You may be reluctant to share your feelings with your partner if you're afraid they'll use that knowledge to hurt or embarrass you. That fear may be based upon a negative experience you've had in a previous relationship, or earlier in your current relationship. You may be afraid to share your feelings if you're embarrassed by those feelings. For example, some men — in particular — may feel that by being open about their fear of failure, or their feelings of inadequacy, that they are not living up to their father's (or society's) expectation that "real men" don't talk about their fears. You may be reluctant to share your feelings if you sense that the feeling is too personal to share with anyone, even your partner.

As an example of how fear can be predicated upon a negative experience, let's say that during an intimate moment you confide to your partner that you're often afraid of not being able to please them in bed. Then, perhaps many months later during an argument, your partner, while trying to hurt you, says out of anger, "You're a lousy lover, you *should* be afraid of not being able to please me." Your partner has betrayed your trust. They've used a highly personal insight into your feelings — which you confided to them — to hurt you.

After this kind of negative experience, it's doubtful that you will be inclined to share another intimate personal feeling with your partner, because they've now used that knowledge to hurt you. Ironically, you'll find — as many of my clients have found — that sometime much later your partner blames you for not being open or willing to communicate your feelings. Then incredibly, they say something like, "I never know what you're feeling. How do you expect me to understand you?"

I can't tell you how often I hear one or both partners complain during dissolution of marriage mediation that "We simply don't communicate." The foregoing is an example of a situation that often occurs with couples who say lack of communication is the primary reason they're dissolving their marriage.

Some men, while they were children, may have been told by their fathers (or father figures) that "real men" don't cry; that "real men" don't act afraid; that "real men" keep things to themselves. I find that interesting, because "real men" *do* emote and are open and vulnerable. Notwithstanding our opinions about "real men," the fact remains that many women are partners with a man who still believes that it's unmanly to share his feelings when it comes to his fears or feelings of inadequacy. For a woman who is partnered with such a man, getting him to talk about anything personal is like pulling teeth. You might try bringing him out of his shell by going back to Part Two of this book and getting him to talk about his childhood and how he related to his parents, siblings, and so forth. If you don't give up trying to help him share himself with you, he eventually *will* share — and, in doing so, become more fully your best friend.

Then again, many of us have feelings that are so personal that we avoid facing them ourselves, let alone sharing them with someone else. I'm not going to address this kind of failure to share feelings, because these feelings *may* be shared — not only with yourself but also your partner — when you feel secure enough with yourself and in your relationship to do so. When you're able to do this, you are not only being your own best friend but also your partner's best friend forever.

Relationships are always evolving and changing. Sometimes they evolve into healthier, warmer, more loving relationships … and sometimes they change for the worse as each of you hides behind your own barrier. You can guarantee that your relationship will change for the worse if you continue to allow yourself to build these impenetrable barriers, rather than by *clearly and lovingly* expressing the pain you feel when your partner does something that hurts you, and explain to them how their words or actions make you feel. You must be open and express your feelings.

■ FAILING TO MAKE GOOD EYE CONTACT

When you fail to make good eye contact, you're not allowing your partner to hear everything you want to say. When you allow your partner to look into your eyes to see the expression, to see the feeling, to read in your eyes the meaning of the words they're hearing, you allow them to understand what you're trying to express in words. You allow them to see your feelings. You allow them to see your fear. You allow them to see your comfort.

On the other hand, when you don't make good eye contact,

you shut them out. They are unable to hear everything they need to hear so they can understand you. The effect of failing to make good eye contact — which limits your partner's ability to hear you — can best be compared to speaking on the telephone with a connection so bad only your every fourth word can be heard. As your partner is listening to your every fourth word, they are saying, "I don't understand you. I can't hear you. You're phasing in and out. Please, let me hear all of your words. Call me back so I can better hear what you're trying to say to me."

When you are not making good eye contact, you should assume that your partner is only hearing a fraction of what you're saying. In addition to not being able to hear, your partner also gets the feeling that you're shutting them out. And every time your eyes are not in direct contact with your partner's — so that both of you can exchange all of the openness and insights you should be exchanging — it's as if a barrier has dropped down between you. That barrier prevents your partner from clearly hearing, seeing, or feeling you. Clear communication is impossible.

If you're experiencing a relationship with a partner whose eye contact is not good, next time you're with them, reach out and touch their face gently with your hand and move their head so their eyes directly align with yours. Then say to them, "Darling, I need you to be looking at my eyes when I'm talking to you because I want you to really hear me; I want you to understand all the feelings that go with the words so that you are hearing me as clearly as possible." You'll probably need to continually do that with your partner until their eye contact improves.

If you or your partner fail to make good eye contact with one another, you shut each other out. Although this *is* another abandonment-causing behavior, it perhaps is not as serious as others. When it happens, maybe only "pieces" of those bricks are added to one's barrier, but don't kid yourself — piece after piece, year after year, can still add up to a lot of bricks, and that barrier still gets bigger.

■ PUTTING YOUR PARTNER FIRST

This next statement cannot be said often enough. It is that important. While you're with your partner — alone or with other members of your family, whether it is before work, after work, or on weekends — you *must* pay attention to every possible aspect of your partner and your relationship with your partner. That may mean a gentle kiss, or bringing them a cup of coffee, or cuddling with them in the morning or in front of the TV at night. It may be that you take time to notice things about your partner that will enable you to anticipate your partner's needs. It could be any number of the things you do. But you have to remember that *nothing* is more important than putting your relationship with your partner above everything else. Without that great relationship, you may not be able to be your best in every other aspect of your life.

You must also remember that when you come home at night from work, regardless of whatever went on during the day at work, you must leave that behind you when you walk in the house. Although it is important to experience personal growth in terms of your career, you must not let it interfere with dedication to being your partner's best friend.

■ TIME TO REFLECT

Just for a moment, let's look back at all the other forms of abandonment-causing behaviors and take moments from each. For example, from one segment you say something that causes your partner to feel unworthy like, "you're stupid." From another you compare your partner to another person of the same sex; from another abuse drugs or alcohol, you interrupt, or you spend too much time with your friends; and from one other you yell at your partner. You have all of these abandonment-causing behaviors and each one results in a brick or two added to your partner's barrier every month or so.

These behaviors begin to take their toll. Barriers keep getting higher and thicker. You become more defensive as a result of it, and before you know it, you're truly not on the same page together, and you are disagreeing with each other about too many things. You begin not accepting your partner as they are and you want to change them into the person you *wish* they were. As the trend continues, it picks up speed. Before you know it, you both are behind a huge, thick barrier — and there is nothing going on between you.

You hear yourselves say, "We don't have anything in common" although that may not be the case. You may still have a lot in common. You still both want to be held, be loved, be caressed, and share good and bad times together — but there's little or no positive interaction between the two of you. There's no positive connection because you are both hiding from each other behind your protective barriers.

That's pretty much what's happened with relationships that have failed or are in the process of failing. It may not have been one particular thing that has caused that barrier to be built. As you're reading on through this part of the book in particular, remember that you need to maintain a high awareness level so you don't allow abandonment-causing behaviors to creep into your repertoire of how you interact with your partner. It's really important to understand that it is this *awareness level* you need to bring to your relationship.

This little "editorial" has been interjected so that you now can begin to focus on why relationships fail. They fail because both partners don't have high enough awareness levels; because they are distracted by the difficulties of living life every day. This distraction takes our attention from the one really important thing that should come before everything else: to have a partner with whom you can peacefully travel this wonderful, yet difficult journey of life.

CHAPTER 11

CHAUVINISTIC BEHAVIOR

■ EXPECTING TO BE SERVICED IN BED

How gross! This is a horribly selfish thing to do to your partner. The right to make love to your partner is earned by being their best friend. It is earned by not perpetuating abandonment-causing behavior. When you expect to be serviced in bed, your partner feels you are so self-centered that you believe they are obligated to perform sexual favors for you. *No one* is obligated to perform sexual favors for another person — and the belief that one *is* obligated is an abusive behavior. It is as abusive as hitting your partner. It is as abusive as verbally assaulting your partner. It's just another way of doing it. Your partner doesn't feel loved. There's no pleasure in giving when there's an expectation that there is an obligation that must be fulfilled.

If you expect to be serviced in bed, you are neither being a loving respectful partner nor a best friend. If that is your expectation, you can be assured that your partner is doing only that: servicing you in bed. They are not making love to you. They are not giving of themselves freely and comfortably. They don't want to share that special feeling of being in love in every possible way by making love to you.

There's a huge difference between being "serviced" and being made love to. If you're expecting to be serviced in bed, you are conveying the message to your partner that they are there not because you want to share an intimate experience with them, but only to bring you to climax.

If you expect to be serviced in bed, it's as if you sat down and said to your partner: "Now listen to me. This is your job — just like cooking for me, like washing my clothes for me, or folding my underwear and putting it away neatly in my drawer. When you get into bed with me, it's a job just like those jobs and I expect you to do it properly. You are to do anything I ask you to do, any-time I ask you to do it. You have to make sure that I reach climax any time I want and as many times as I want. You are expected to allow me to do anything to you — no matter how demeaning it may be. You are expected to act as though you enjoy it."

Those words, of course, are probably not ever said quite this way, but they don't have to be spoken. If you are expecting to be serviced in bed, that expectation conveys those words loud and clear to your partner. You are also conveying another message to your partner: "I'm expecting you to service me the way I want to be serviced. I don't care whether you feel like a prostitute while you're doing it. I don't care whether you are receiving any enjoy-ment while you are in bed with me. I don't care whether you are disgusted by the process. I don't care whether you feel unworthy while you're performing the acts I'm demanding you perform. I don't care whether you feel one moment's pleasure or whether you like me, let alone love me. This is what I'm demanding, and if you don't do it, I will get rid of you."

If you are the person who is servicing your partner in bed, it's as if you are saying to yourself: "I am not worthy of being with a person who feels wonderful about me. I am not worthy of being treated in a sensuous, loving manner. I am servicing this person because I need something from them; I need to be sup-ported by them."

If you're the one expecting to be serviced in bed, your part-ner has built a *huge* barrier that is probably impenetrable. The pain that you have caused your partner is probably so great that they can't bear to be near you. Again, as we've said in other sections of this chapter, your partner may be going through the motions of being with you, but they are not really with you in the way that best friends are with each other. In all likelihood, your relationship is over unless for some strange reason, you suddenly understood the pain you've caused your partner to feel, and beg for the forgiveness of your partner.

■ FAILING TO TAKE RESPONSIBILITY FOR MISTAKES

"I didn't do it." "It wasn't me." "It was no big deal." "It was your fault, not mine." These are the words of a person who fails to take responsibility for mistakes.

"Yes, it was me, I screwed up." "I'm sorry, I shouldn't have done it. I was having a bad day, and I used poor judgement. I'll be careful not to let it happen again." These are the words of a person who takes responsibility for mistakes.

It doesn't matter how careful you are about things we do each day. We all make mistakes. It can't be helped. Our minds wander. We become tired. We're concentrating on other things. We didn't anticipate a problem that we might have protected against if we had been paying better attention or we simply use bad judgement. It happens to all of us.

Failing to accept responsibility for your mistakes is the same as not telling the truth. It's the same as not being open and vulnerable with your partner. It's the same as trying to pretend you are someone or something you're not. Since all of us make mistakes, it should be easy to be able to accept the fact that your partner has acknowledged that they've made a mistake; forgive them, and move on. However, when your partner tries to cover up a mistake, make excuses, or pretend it didn't happen, you resent their lack of honesty. It is that lack of openness and honesty that causes your partner to add a brick to their barrier and experience anxiety.

It's unnecessary to spend a lot of time on this topic. Your partner wants to love you, wants to believe you, and wants to forgive you — because they know that they, too, make mistakes and will want acceptance and forgiveness when they acknowledge their mistakes. Just do it!

■ FAILING TO RESPECT A PARTNER'S PERSPECTIVE

When you are involved in a relationship with your best friend, there can never be a time when one of you is right and the other one is wrong. If there is a time — or many times — in your relationship that you take the position that your partner is wrong, you are not respecting your partner's feelings or perspective. When you do this, you shut your partner out of the decision-making process. If your partner feels that you don't respect their perspective, then they believe that you don't respect *them*; and if they believe that you don't respect *them*, they won't feel loved. They will add another brick to their barrier and react in a negative way that creates conflict between the two of you.

Recently I mediated the dissolution of marriage for Paul and Ellen. Paul is a very large man in stature, standing over six feet tall and weighing almost 300 pounds, while Ellen is petite and just over five feet tall. Ellen's biggest complaint is that Paul believes he is always right about everything and doesn't respect Ellen's opinion.

During my first meeting with Paul and Ellen, I asked each of them what they believed the primary issues were of their pending dissolution of marriage. Ellen said she believed the primary issue was custody of their two young children. When Paul heard Ellen state her opinion, he immediately shot back, "Ellen doesn't know what she's talking about, we've already made a decision about custody."

When Ellen heard Paul repeat the same sort of demeaning words she had been hearing for the last eight years, she became very agitated and said, "There, that's exactly why I don't want to be married to him any longer."

Ellen has an opinion. It doesn't matter if her perspective is correct or not. It's her perspective — and for Paul to be her best friend, he must respect it. He doesn't have to agree with it, but he does have to acknowledge that it's her perspective and either modify *his* perspective to coincide with Ellen's, or realize and accept the fact that winning any battle of who is right or wrong is not important. It's not only not important, it's counterproductive. In the overall scheme of things, what is more important than loving, trusting, sharing, and enjoying life — peaceful, satisfying life — together with your partner? Does it really matter, for example, where you go to dinner, or whether your daughter takes ballet or modern jazz classes? Does it really matter if the car is blue or white; Chevrolet or Ford?

When we acknowledge each other's perspectives as correct — even if we don't necessarily agree with them — we each move a little bit toward some center point; some common ground. It's really easy to say, "OK, honey, sure, no problem" over the minor disagreements that occur during any relationship. If you do respect your partner's perspective, you'll be kissed, hugged, and loved that night because you made your partner's life slightly easier that day by not trying to overpower them.

■ FAILING TO TREAT PARTNER AS EQUAL

When you and your partner are best friends, the topic of failing to treat your partner as an equal is never an issue. It wouldn't ever occur to your partner that you should be subservient because they earn more money. It wouldn't ever occur to you that they are not as smart as you because you earned your degree at a four-year college and they graduated from a community college or high school. In discussing this topic, remember that I'm reflecting on an abandonment-causing behavior, a behavior that causes one partner or the other to experience pain, which in turn causes them to add another brick to their barrier.

I'm sure you've all experienced a moment when you've been in the presence of someone who acts, if only subtly, superior to you. When we refer to a subtle behavior, it may only be that they seem slightly bored being in your presence, or perhaps their nostrils flare just a little, or they spend just a little too much time talking about their accomplishments or what they've bought recently. And the fact may be that they *are* better educated, or have a better job, or are better looking. They may *have* more friends, or live in a bigger house and drive a more expensive car. But who appointed *them* king or queen of the universe and gave them the right to directly or indirectly judge themselves as being superior to you?

It's bad enough, even for a brief moment, being in someone's presence who treats you as though you're not their equal. But being in a *relationship* with someone who thinks they are better than you and therefore expects you to be their "beck and call" person is intolerable. "Bring me a beer." "Get me my dinner." "Answer the phone." "Drive the kids." "Write the checks." "Why aren't my clothes washed, folded, and in my closet?"

When someone treats you as though you are not their equal, and expects you to be their servant, each order they give may be followed, initially at least. But, make no mistake about it, another brick is added to their partner's barrier — and complete protection from the hurt that partner fees is not far away.

■ FAILING TO SHARE IN HOUSEHOLD RESPONSIBILITIES

Years ago, it was a woman's job to clean the house, do the wash, and bear the primary responsibility for preparing dinner. It was the man's job to go out into the big, bad world and earn a living so that he could support his family. Now, both men and women share equally in the responsibilities of meeting household responsibilities and earning a living. It is not only unreasonable, but also *selfish* for a man to expect his partner to carry a full-time job and be responsible for doing all of the things she used to be responsible for when she *didn't* work outside the home.

Men, if you're coming home from work being fully exhausted and expecting to have dinner on the table waiting for you… if you're expecting the house to be spotless… if you're expecting to have your clothes washed, ironed, and placed carefully in your drawers and closet, you'd better be earning a few hundred thousand dollars each year so that you can afford a full-time maid. Otherwise — unless you're sharing absolutely equally in every aspect of taking care of your personal needs at home — you had best not be saying things like "The house is a mess," "I'm starved, why isn't dinner ready?," or "I don't have any clean underwear." And even if you *are* sharing equally in every aspect of taking care of your needs at home, you'd be much better off not using words like those anyway because your partner will assume you mean it's her fault that those things aren't done and she will resent the implication.

In almost every dissolution of marriage case that I mediate, in addition to partners being guilty of many other abandonment-causing behaviors, I see that barriers were built because men "expected" their women partners to be responsible for the household stuff. The cry of being "taken for granted" is an oft-heard one. There is one thing that women must be aware of, however, and that is they must not start out a relationship by trying to prove that they are superhuman and convey the impression that they can both work full-time outside of the house *and* do all the cooking, cleaning, and so forth.

Women need to remember that men, as little boys, learned that mom will take care of them. It's easy for them to expect that their partner will always do the same. Ground rules must be established from the beginning concerning the sharing of household responsibilities. Otherwise, the barriers that women build may be, in part, to protect themselves from the anger they feel toward themselves for trying to prove that they are sufficiently competent to carry two full-time jobs. They are setting themselves up to allow their man or partner to sit and watch them work themselves into a state of exhaustion while he watches a basketball, baseball, or football game after work because "he worked soooo hard that day."

■ BEING PATRONIZING

If you are conveying the impression to your partner that your job is more important or harder to do than their job, you're setting yourself up for failure in your relationship. If you're a female doctor, for example, and your male partner is a teacher, even the slightest indication that you're smarter or more successful because you earn a higher income will cause him to add another brick to his barrier. If you're a male vice-president of a major corporation and your female partner is an Avon representative, the same thing is true.

We all know that you have achieved a terrific goal; that you worked for years to become a doctor or a vice-president. Your partner respects you for achieving those goals, too. You don't have to attempt to make yourself feel more successful by patronizing your partner and making them feel *less* successful. Each time you convey even the slightest impression that your partner's job is a "cute little thing for them to be doing," your partner is adding another of those disgusting little bricks to their barrier. Remember this: if you're smart enough to have earned a medical degree or achieved some other high-level position, you're smart and secure enough not to allow your partner to think for even a moment that you feel superior to them. Saying you're sorry after the "bell has rung" won't work. The damage will have been done, and if it continues to happen, you're relationship will soon be done, too.

CHAPTER 12

UNTRUSTWORTHY BEHAVIOR

■ BEING DISHONEST

There's probably not any one abandonment-causing behavior that makes your partner feel more abandoned than any other — but listen loud and clear to this one. You *must* tell the truth about everything, even the smallest detail, if you want to be your partner's best friend. In order to help you understand why this is so important, I'd like to tell you about Janice and Kent, for whom I mediated a dissolution of marriage about four years ago.

Janice was only 20 when she met Kent. She was a senior in college, majoring in fashion design. Kent was 29 years old and owned his own clothing manufacturing business, which was in its third year of operation. Kent had attended college, but did not graduate — he left school and began selling a woman's line of clothing when he finished his junior year.

By Janice's own admission, she was easily snowed by Kent. He was handsome, he owned a business in her field of interest, he drove a 450SL Mercedes, he dressed great, and he was charming. They met in a fashionable woman's clothing store where Janice was looking at a line of clothing that Kent's company had manufactured. Janice was impressed and, as she said, would have believed anything Kent told her.

Although Kent had a flare for choosing the right designers for whom to manufacture, and although the quality of his manufacturing was excellent, Kent frequently underestimated his cost to manufacture goods, failed to accurately include fixed overhead costs into his estimates, and his company was losing about $10,000 each month.

Kent always expected to generate that "really big order" that would put him over the top, and although he did continue to pull rabbits out of the hat — so to speak — each time he was desperate and needed a big order, it was never enough. The interest drain on the debt he had accumulated, along with his inaccurate manufacturing projections, caused his business to continually lose money.

Janice and Kent fell head over heals in love with each other. Kent bought lavish gifts for Janice. He took her to the finest restaurants. He took her on vacations to Hawaii and Mexico. He often bought new clothes for them both. He did not discuss his business with Janice, other than to tell her which major stores had placed orders with him.

When Kent asked Janice to marry him, she was ecstatic. Kent was the man of her dreams…or so she thought. They were married and they moved into a new apartment in the wealthiest part of town to start their new life.

After they were married, Kent insisted that Janice not open his credit card bills or letters from credit card companies. He became secretive about his business. He continued to reassure her that his business was doing just fine — although in reality it was still struggling.

Janice didn't bother to get a job after she and Kent were married. She instead chose to take a few courses at the university located near their home. Janice never believed, even for a moment, that Kent wasn't making enough money to support them in the lifestyle to which she had become accustomed during their eight-month romance.

One Wednesday afternoon she was at home preparing dinner for Kent, and there was a knock at her front door. It was Sandy, the manager of the apartment building. Sandy first asked if Kent was at home, and when Janice said "No," Sandy handed Janice an eviction notice. Janice told Sandy that there must have been a mistake, because she was sure that Kent would have paid the rent on their apartment. Sandy told Janice that the rent hadn't been paid for two months. Janice said that Kent had been extremely busy and that it must have slipped his mind and that as soon as Kent came home he would bring a check to her.

When Kent came home, Janice sheepishly handed the eviction notice to Kent. Kent looked surprised, and then became angry and said that the management company had screwed up their account — he had paid the rent each month exactly on time. As a matter of fact, he said that he had paid a month in advance, and he would take care of it in the morning.

Janice felt better after Kent's explanation, but she was beginning to feel anxious about Kent's secretiveness about his business, the fact that he wouldn't let her look at credit card bills, and now this eviction notice. Janice had previously suppressed her feelings, which she now began to recognize as distrust, about Kent's wanting to handle all of their financial affairs. But now she couldn't overlook the possibility that Kent had not been telling her the truth.

Late the following day, Janice went over to Sandy's office and asked if Kent had paid the rent. She was told that he had. Janice didn't ask if there had been a mistake. First, she didn't want to embarrass Kent if he simply had not paid the rent and second, she didn't want to know if Kent had lied to her. She was afraid that if he had lied about the apartment rent being paid that he could be lying about other things, too.

Things seemed to be unravelling in Kent's business life. When he came home from work — which began to be later and later each evening — he complained of how the economy was depressed and that his customers weren't paying him on time so that he could pay his suppliers as he had agreed. It seemed that every little thing Janice did made Kent angry, and he would yell at her — "Don't you understand how much pressure I'm under?" — and then apologize and try to explain why his business was failing. Janice would become angry, too; she would yell back and say things like, "You never tell me anything — how do I know what's really going on?"

Kent was still getting home from work about 6:15 or so each evening, but one evening, when Janice glanced at the clock and it was 6:45 p.m., she began to worry. She called Kent's office and there was no answer. She called his cellular phone and she found that he was either out of range or it was turned off. She then decided to call Maxwell & Sons, Kent's largest account, to see if maybe he had stopped there. She spoke with Morrie Maxwell, the senior partner, and although they had a nice friendly conversation, Morrie said that Kent hadn't stopped by for about a week.

About five minutes after Janice hung up the phone, Kent walked in looking disheveled. His tie was just hanging around his neck, his pants were wrinkled, and he looked kind of spaced out. It was about 7:15 p.m. Janice said, "Hi, honey — how come you're home so late? I was worried about you." Kent explained that he stopped by some of his accounts on the way home to pick up checks and his last stop was Morrie Maxwell, and "...you know how Morrie likes to talk." He then went into the bathroom to clean up.

Janice didn't know what to do. Should she tell Kent that she knew he didn't see Morrie? Should she pretend nothing was wrong? Or should she stay calm and try to initiate conversation about her concerns about their business and their lack of communication in order to try to get Kent to open up?

Janice was clearly worried. Bills weren't being paid. Kent's business was in trouble, and he wouldn't discuss anything pertaining to it with her. He appeared to have lied about the rent being paid, and now she knew he had not told her the truth about why he was late. Was he having an affair? Was he spending money on another woman?

Let's stop for just a moment and take a look at the dynamics of this relationship.

From the beginning of the relationship, Kent pretended to be a responsible, successful businessman earning a great deal of money. He lied. Janice believed him, though, and placed her trust in him to take care of their financial affairs. She loved being wined and dined, and she loved having a man buy her presents and take her wonderful places. It was easy to trust him; to sit back and let all those wonderful things happen to her.

But after they got married, Kent's secrecy about his business and about their personal financial affairs made Janice feel separated from Kent. She became slightly afraid and she began to add a few bricks to a barrier she started to build when he wouldn't let her open the mail or when he wouldn't answer her questions about finances. She continued to build her barrier — a little more quickly when the manager of the apartment building delivered an eviction notice. This barrier became slightly higher each day, when Kent became irritable with her no matter what she did. Kent was clearly angry at himself for lying to Janice and he was projecting the anger he felt at himself at her.

Janice, in the meantime, began withdrawing from Kent as her barrier became higher and higher. She wasn't as affectionate with him as she had been. She didn't feel as comfortable sharing herself with him in all the ways she had done before. And she was yelling at him more, too — because she was angry at herself for abdicating all the household financial affairs to him and not checking out his "successful image" before she married him. Now she was projecting the anger she felt towards herself at him, too.

Since you already know I mediated a dissolution of marriage for this couple, you can pretty much guess the rest of the story. No, Kent wasn't having an affair. He was going to the race track late in the afternoon, and losing money. Kent and Janice started to argue even more, and both of them attacked the other. Kent blamed the fact that their marriage was on the rocks on Janice, claiming that she had never been supportive. All she did, he said, was buy clothes, clothes, and more clothes. Janice, of course, claimed Kent was someone who couldn't tell the truth about anything and who had a gambling addiction. Eventually, Kent closed the business, filed for bankruptcy, and then had an affair. Janice moved into an apartment with a girlfriend, and filed for divorce.

Barriers are built by each of us for many reasons, but none get built faster by your partner than if you don't tell the truth about everything. You see, if you don't tell the truth to your partner about even the smallest detail, you can't feel good about yourself. If you don't feel good about yourself, you build your own barrier — which separates you from your partner as well as your true self. If you don't love yourself because you know you aren't telling the truth, you can't love your partner the way they need to be loved.

If your partner senses that you are not telling the truth about everything, they feel anxious — although they may not be exactly sure *why* they feel anxious. If they feel anxious, they begin building a barrier, which is intended to protect them from whatever it is they're afraid of. If they are afraid that their partner is not telling them the truth about everything, their fear stems from being afraid of what the truth may really be, being afraid that the connection they thought was there with their partner is not really there, being afraid of not having someone to love, being afraid of losing the person they love, and being afraid that they made an error in judgement when they entered into the relationship. The tension created by this fear undermines the peacefulness a couple must maintain if they are to remain best friends forever.

Tell the truth about *everything* — even the smallest detail. We all know when someone is not telling the truth. Woman especially know when their man is not being honest. Among all the abandonment-causing behaviors, this is truly an important one. Telling the truth keeps the foundation of the relationship solid. Even when a relationship becomes a little unstable from time to time, if each of you continues to tell the truth about *everything* — including your own feelings — I think you have a really good chance to remain best friends and lovers. We all need someone to love. We all need to be loved. Loving someone who you can trust to always tell you the truth, no matter what, feels safe. And feeling safe is the beginning of "forever."

PART
FOUR

Keys to
a Good
Relationship

CHAPTER 13

LITTLE THINGS MEAN A LOT

■ ANTICIPATING NEEDS

It's not too difficult to see everything you need to hear about your partner.

Yes, you read it right — *see* everything you need to *hear*. When it involves your best friend, you must be able to recognize what they're thinking and feeling from the look on their face, expression in their eyes, quick glance in one direction or another, briskness of their step, knowledge of the time of day, knowledge of where they've been or are going, the feel of their kiss, or the touch of their hand. You should be able to tell if they are relaxed or tense, feeling positive or slightly negative, tired or rested, and happy or sad. You should be able to tell if they need you to do something for them or need to be left alone. You must be able to anticipate the needs of your partner if you are going to earn the right to truly be their best friend.

I can't begin to count the number of times that I've heard a man say, "...but I can't read her mind." The truth is that men *must* be able to read their partner's mind if they hope to be their partner forever. Women expect it. Women need it.

Most women test their man at least once each day — or every other day — to find out if he "gets it," at least until they're sure he does.

Since you presumably spend more time with your partner than you do with any other person, you need to sense everything they're feeling by just being in their presence. You should only have to glance in their direction for a moment or two to be able to see what's going on with them.

Here's an example of what I mean by maintaining a heightened level of awareness.

You're in the kitchen, having come home from work a little early, drinking a glass of wine, and reading the morning paper that you haven't had a chance to read all day. Your partner comes home from work. It's 5:45 p.m. and she's about 20 minutes later than normal. She says her boss needed her to assemble some information for tomorrow's board of directors meeting, so she couldn't leave on time. She's the one who normally is responsible for preparing dinner. On occasion you help by preparing dinner, too — although this time you didn't think of doing it. She's holding two bags of groceries. You can see through the kitchen window that she's left the car door open, as she was carrying too many things to close it, and there are still some grocery bags in the car. You hear your daughter Sara call out from her bedroom, "Mommy, is that you?" You can see her sigh just slightly as she hears Sara's words. She glances at the mail quickly as she passes the small desk in the kitchen.

What do you know about what your best friend is feeling?

She's feeling somewhat anxious because she's later than normal and dinner isn't ready for you.

She feeling overburdened because she feels that she hasn't been available for Sara or you, yet she knows she's been extremely busy all day at work.

She's exhausted.

She doesn't want to ask you to help because she hopes you'll see for yourself that she needs your help.

Sara is her first priority. She needs to kiss her first and at least tell her that mommy will be with her in a few minutes.

She knows the laundry needs to be done (it always needs to

be done), dinner has to be made, and the groceries have to be put away. She can't wait to get out of her work clothes and into something comfortable. She hopes you'll understand that she's sorry she's late, that she doesn't feel like a good wife because dinner's not ready for you, she feels as though she looks like a mess, and — oh my God I forgot to kiss him.

Men, don't just sit there reading your paper — and don't complain that she hasn't asked you how your day was yet. Within seconds of seeing her open the door to the car to get the bags of groceries, this is how you should react:

Take the grocery bags out of her arms and tell her you'll bring the rest in. (She thinks, "Thank God!") Bring in all the groceries and begin putting them away. After she's kissed Sara, she comes into the kitchen and begins helping you.

You finish putting the groceries away and tell her that you'll make Sara a tuna sandwich and that ordering out would be perfect for you. (She says, "No, it'll only take me a moment to prepare dinner.") You say, "A baked potato, cottage cheese, and some sliced tomatoes would be perfect — and I'll get it ready." About this time, you walk over to her, put your arms around her, and hold her for a moment. (She'll only let it be for a moment because she remembers the laundry needs to be done.) Sara calls out for her again, and you tell her to go to Sara.

Once again she knows that you are anticipating her needs, understanding her thoughts without her having to express them, and that you are truly her best friend.

And what about *me*, you ask? What do *I* get for being her best friend? The answer is — exactly the same, only ten times more. Just anticipate her needs regularly and see what happens.

■ BE CLEAN, SMELL GOOD

From time to time while writing this book I've wondered how much of what I'm saying is common sense or real insight. Do we really have to say that each of us needs to be clean and smell good? For example, don't we all know that, at least in part, the reason we are attracted to someone is that it feels good to be in their presence, and that it feels that way because they are not lazy when it comes to their personal hygiene.

Allen and Beth came to me in late 1996 because Beth wanted to dissolve their marriage. Allen wanted to go to counseling, but Beth wanted to end it. I met with them both together at first, and Beth said that she was sure that Allen didn't love her because he didn't care about her feelings and about what was important to her. For example, she said, "I know Allen works hard and sometimes he has to work late. But he *never* asks about my day. He never asks if my day was a hard one or interesting." Beth also commented that Allen had to have control of the money. If *he* wanted something he could buy it — but she had to ask him for money if she wanted to buy something.

Allen once again reiterated that he loved Beth and didn't want this divorce. He didn't have any complaints except that she didn't kiss him often enough and didn't want to make love to him except for once or twice each month, when he almost had to beg for it.

Something didn't feel right. Beth's reasons for wanting to dissolve their marriage seemed easily remedied. There was no domestic violence. Allen rarely yelled at Beth. Allen provided a good living for their family and Beth was able to be the primary caretaker of their children. Neither one of them had been unfaithful. I was sure that I wasn't hearing the complete story. Had Beth fallen in love with another man? I asked to meet with each one of them alone, and Beth volunteered to be first.

I started by asking Beth, "What's really going on here? This picture doesn't seem complete. Why are you *really* wanting to dissolve this marriage?" Beth started by asking if everything she said in mediation was confidential. I explained that it was, and that I could not be subpoenaed to testify at trial if mediation wasn't successful. Beth then went on to say that Allen didn't shower or shave often enough, and that he smelled badly most of the time. I asked if she had *told* him that he didn't smell good, and she said she had, but that he wouldn't do anything about it. I asked if that was really the primary reason for her wanting to divorce Allen, and she said that she just couldn't go through life not being able to stand the way he smelled.

I asked Beth to sit in the lobby for a few minutes while I spoke with Allen.

When Allen came back into my office I asked him what he thought the real reason was that Beth wanted a divorce. He said that he didn't have any idea. I then told him what Beth had told me. He couldn't believe that the reason she wanted a divorce was that he didn't shower and shave enough. I told him that wasn't the real reason. I said, "It's because you smell. She just couldn't tell you how strongly she felt about it." I offered this suggestion to him: "Go home and take a shower. Be sure to shower in the morning every day before work and at night before you go to sleep. Shave each time you shower, too.

I asked Beth to come back into the office and I set an appointment for them to begin mediation the following week.

Yep, you guessed it.

The day before the appointment, Beth called and cancelled the appointment. She said "Allen is clean and smells good all the time now — I can't believe I ever thought of spending my life without him." I haven't heard from Beth and Allen since that call, but I'm betting that Allen's not complaining any longer about not being kissed by Beth enough.

■ CREATING PEACEFULNESS

One of the primary goals of being your partner's best friend is to help your partner maintain as low a level of anxiety as possible. I'm not suggesting here that you are responsible for the mental health of your partner. I am saying, though, that you need to be aware of those things that give your partner anxiety and be sure that *you* are not the cause of any such anxiety.

Here are a few examples of things that probably will create anxiety in your partner:

- Monthly bills are not paid on time and you hide bills that are not paid.
- Credit cards are used irresponsibly and without your partner's knowledge.
- You take out credit cards without your partner's knowledge.
- You quit your job without first discussing it with your partner.
- You're not responsible at work.
- You don't tell your partner the total truth about everything.
- You don't tell your partner where you are going or when you'll be back.
- You drive faster than feels comfortable to your partner.
- You make turns into oncoming traffic that are slightly risky.
- You drink or abuse alcohol and drive.
- You fall asleep when you are responsible for watching your children.
- You don't follow through on details.
- You are critical of your partner's behavior.
- You are often late getting to work or for appointments.
- You rush your partner when the two of you are getting ready to go somewhere.
- You don't file your tax returns on time and don't pay your taxes.
- You don't maintain a life insurance policy on yourself.
- You don't maintain a membership in an automobile club.
- You exaggerate to your friends.
- You pay too much attention to someone of the opposite sex.
- You don't admit a mistake.
- You break any law.
- You don't maintain good eye contact with your partner.
- You interrupt your partner.
- You often allow yourself to be interrupted when your partner is speaking to you.

- You make negative statements to your partner and to others about your partner.
- You don't create and follow a monthly budget.
- You stay on-line too much.
- You go into chat rooms when you could be sharing time with your partner.
- You correspond through e-mail with someone of the opposite sex too often and you explain that you're "just friends."
- You allow the tires on your car to become too worn.
- You go out with your friends more than you do with your partner.
- You don't maintain a retirement plan.
- You do and say embarrassing things in public.

When your partner experiences anxiety they are not free to be completely open. They are not free to feel the warmth of your love or the joy of your children. They are not free to become all that they were intended to become or enjoy the beauty in their life. Help them to remain clear of the blocks that encumber our being when we have anxiety.

Here are a few positive things you can do that will help your partner to remain peaceful:

- While cuddling with your partner in the morning, place your hand the middle of their back and allow it to rest peacefully. Allow your partner to feel the peacefulness of your mind transfer through your arm and hand and into their body. Imagine that peacefulness spreads throughout your partner's entire body. Imagine it cleanses and soothes your partner's every organ, artery, and blood vessel. Imagine that this peacefulness soothes your partner's very being. Then place a long, slow, soft kiss on your partner's back exactly where you had placed your hand.
- Before leaving for work hold your partner tightly but gently, placing your hand in the middle of their back and pressing their body close to yours.

- Hold your partner's face in your two hands and kiss them gently on the mouth and face.
- Maintain perfect eye contact with your partner when they are talking to you, or you to them.
- Say "thank you" to your partner often. Let them know that you are aware of every positive thing that they do for you.
- Do the opposite of everything listed above under examples of "things that will probably create anxiety."
- Tell your partner to "be safe" before they leave in a car to go anywhere.
- Give *more* than 50 per cent.

How often have we heard that maintaining a good partnership takes "work"…that it's a 50–50 proposition? I don't believe that is true.

It doesn't take work. It's fun. It's easy. Every day can be perfect. But you have to pay *100 percent* attention to your best friend every day for it to be fun, easy, and perfect.

■ MAKE LOVE FROM SUNRISE TO SUNSET

If you've read this book up to this point, I hope I have helped you understand how to be best friends forever. Here, however, I'll let you see how best friends make love from sunrise to sunset. (It's just an example of how best friends may go through one day.)

He awakes before her and he takes the time he needs to do "his things." She's gotten the coffee-maker ready the night before, so all he has to do is flip the switch. When it's time to awaken his partner, he crawls into bed beside her. He cuddles close and begins to gently rub her back. He scratches her back a little, too. He entwines his feet with hers.

After she opens her eyes and sits up, he brings her a cup of coffee. She turns on *Good Morning America* and sips her coffee slowly. He makes the children's lunches because she's running a little late. She puts in a load of laundry.

He begins to get dressed and, as usual, she has made sure that he has fresh underwear and socks to put on. She gets into the shower while he eats his breakfast. His bananas and strawberries are nearly always there for him. As he hears the shower stop, he gets up from the kitchen table and brings the coffee pot so he can warm up her coffee. She's wrapped in a towel, dripping wet, but always remembers to say "thank you." He empties the dishwasher because she doesn't like to do it. He leaves a little extra cash by her purse.

As she comes into the kitchen after drying off and putting on her robe, he says he's going to leave for work. They speak for a moment about things each will do and he holds her tightly for a second and kisses her gently. He says, "Be safe, my love." She says, "Pay attention, too, please."

They go their separate ways, each being diligent about their job. Each feeling loved. About noon or so, she calls him to ask how he is. Sometimes he calls her just to hear her voice. They just need to hear that the other is okay.

She stops to pick up the laundry and a few things from the market and gets home before he does. She folds the laundry, starts something for dinner and checks on the kids. He calls to say he's leaving work and tells her the time he'll be home. He walks in the house within 5 minutes or so of when he said he would. He looks around, knows everyone is home and takes a deep breath, a sigh of relief that everyone is safe.

He says, "Hi, honey. How was your day?" She listens to him. He listens to her. She always looks great. It doesn't matter what she's got on or whether she's even had time to freshen up a little after work. As he walks by her on his way to the bedroom to change his clothes, he brushes the back of his hand over her hips. She says, "Dinner will be ready soon."

She brings dinner to him at the kitchen table when it's ready. They eat and talk. He never interrupts, even though he's sure he's heard it before. When they are finished with the meal, he says, "Thank you, it was great." He removes the dishes from the table and helps to wash and put them in the dishwasher. He remembers that she's worked outside the house all day, too.

He does his thing while she does hers, together and individually. She says, "I'm going to take a bath. Do you want to take one afterwards?" He says that he does and when she calls him after her bath, he goes into the bathroom to find a tub full of bubble bath and candles flickering around.

He relaxes in the tub and then gets into bed where more candles are lit and the stereo is sounding. They touch feet and hands as they did early that day. They lie quietly and peacefully without a need to say that the day was a good one that they shared as best friends. But he says once more, "I love you, my love." She fixes his pillow and tucks him in tight as she thinks to herself, "You're a good boy, sleep tight."

We're not suggesting that you don't have sex, too. It's just slightly less significant — but much more fun — when you make love from sunrise to sunset.

■ A WIN FOR YOU IS A WIN FOR ME

Have you ever heard of community property law? Hmmm. Seriously, though, when something great happens to your partner there are many reasons why it's great for you, too. Certainly, we can look at all of the positives that are derived from your partner getting a raise, achieving higher position in their company, or winning an award. If your partner generates more income, it of course benefits you.

Monetary wins are really terrific, but that's not what I'm referring to here. As I've noted previously, when you pass through life with your best friend, any positive upward movement moves you both in that positive direction. You are partners. You are umbilically bound to one another. When your partner is rewarded, the reward is unavoidably shared. When your partner feels proud, you feel proud. You and your partner, although very much individuals and growing separately as individuals, are bound together by your best friend connection. So although you may be proud of "a win," that pride you feel is unavoidably transferred to your best friend and they feel proud, too.

This connection is not one you can visually see. It is one though that you can feel. Try it next time you and your partner feel like making love. No, this time I don't mean "making love" only in the *physical* sense — I mean making love in the *spiritual* sense.

Sit facing each other with your legs crossed. Don't touch one another. No, really — keep your hands off your partner. OK, look deeply into each other's eyes. Feel the connection spread from the look and feel in each other's eyes down your entire body. Let the connection move down your bodies without allowing your eyes to move from each other. Open your hands, palms up, while they're on your lap. Feel your partner's hands touching your hands, even though it's only the "connection" that makes you feel like they're touching. Allow the connection to move down the rest of your body. Hold it. Feel the full power of the connection. Let this connection permeate your entire body. Wait until it is so powerful that you can't stand not touching your partner.

Okay, now you can touch each other physically. Kiss gently. Kiss passionately. Do whatever feels best.

You and your partner are bound as one. A win for you cannot help but be a win for your partner. You are blessed to have your partner. Cherish them. Be proud of and for them. You are best friends forever.

PART
FIVE

Breaking
Down
Barriers

CHAPTER 14

MAKING AMENDS

*S*ome of you have healthy relationships and have not built — or caused to be built — barriers.

Some of you, from time to time, slip a little and do or say something that causes your partner to add a brick or two — which may, if not broken down immediately, become the foundation of a barrier.

Some of you have been the recipient of the early stages of an abandonment-causing behavior.

Many of you, partially or fully, have shut down emotionally, and go through life as if a in dream, not fully experiencing the beauty and satisfaction of sharing all of yourself with your partner.

For those of you who have healthy relationships, appreciate the fact that you are blessed, and let that appreciation be the impetus for maintaining a heightened awareness level to protect and nurture that precious and fragile balance that you've established with your partner.

If you're one of those who slip a little from time to time, you must be sure that when you do or say something that hurts your partner, you quickly recognize what you've done, say you're sorry, and never do it again. You must also remember that *when* you say you're sorry, you must stop whatever you're doing, look deeply into your partner's eyes, hold both of their hands in yours, and — without excuses — say something like, "I am *really* sorry, honey. I just lost it. There's absolutely no excuse for me to have said anything so stupid and hurtful to you. I didn't mean it. It's not true and I promise it will never happen again."

Men, especially — you must remember that you cannot wait more than a day at the most to confess your stupidity. If you wait too long, your partner will add another brick or two to that barrier — just because you missed the urgency of saying something that would hopefully have dissolved the blocks, or perhaps even prevented them from being added in the first place.

Women — men tend to be more forgiving, so you can get away with letting it harbor for a few days and it shouldn't matter too much. But nevertheless, it still needs to be said!

Now, for those of you who have maintained a relationship in which you both have inflicted — and continue to inflict — pain upon each other, but both of you really want to love the other and stay together in a healthy way, there are some ways to break down barriers.

First, counseling may be helpful. Speak with friends and others in your community who may be able to recommend a good therapist or marriage counselor. Interview professionals together. If you're really intent on trying to break down barriers and establish a healthy relationship, this is something you must do together. (The process of searching for help can itself be therapeutic.) After you've found someone with whom you both feel comfortable and safe, make a commitment to each other to work the problem through until your relationship is again warm and loving.

In addition to counseling, you may try a technique that from time to time I use during mediation when there are couples who want to reconcile their relationship. (Remember, however, that I am not a therapist and I don't conduct counseling sessions.)

When my "breaking down barrier exercises" are successful, it's almost magical how the barriers of both partners seem to evaporate into thin air. You *can* do this yourself, though. I'll try to guide you through it.

CHAPTER 15

BREAKING DOWN
BARRIERS EXERCISE

For this exercise you'll need a full-length mirror and a willingness to utilize your most vivid imagination. If you don't have a full-length mirror, go buy an inexpensive one — it's important. When positioning the mirror, lean it against the wall on a slight angle so that you and your partner look thinner. (It's always good to look thinner, especially if you're slightly overweight.)

As far as your vivid imagination is concerned, if you don't have one, I can't help you find one. Just find your own — or you'll likely be in some mediator's or attorney's office wishing you had taken the time to be imaginative.

■ STEP ONE

All right, here we go. Sit down in front of the mirror facing your partner, but on a 45-degree angle to one another and the mirror. You need to be able to see your partner and the mirror at the same time. While looking in the mirror, picture the barriers that each of you have built that protect you from the hurt each of you has inflicted on the other. While you're sitting, the barriers start at the floor and come up to just about eye level. Imagine that you can see above the barriers, though, if you sit up slightly straighter. We want you to be able to look into your partner's eyes. Picture the barriers as thick as you imagine your barriers actually are.

Imagine that each brick contains the pain you felt each time your partner made you feel abandoned by his or her behavior. Take your time. Look at the barriers. Feel the pain that each brick contains. Don't block it. Let the pain be excruciating. Allow yourself to cry if you feel like crying. For now, though, if your partner begins to cry, don't reach out to touch them. Sit in this position for as long as you both need. Touch your partner's hand gently with your hand when you have allowed yourself to feel your pain for as long as you need. Do not speak to each other during this first step. When you're both ready to move on to the next step, do so.

■ STEP TWO

Now, adjust your position so that you are facing one another.

Although you're sitting only about three feet apart, do not reach out to touch each other. Sit as upright as each of you can and imagine that you are peering over each of your respective barriers. Gaze into each other's eyes. Eye contact here is critical, even more so than it is normally. Without verbally speaking a word to each other, express your sorrow for the hurt you've caused your partner. Tell your partner, through the sincerity in your eyes, how sad you are that you've hurt them. Tell them that you will never, ever, do anything that will cause them to feel anxiety, or to feel unworthy or unloved. This step should take about five minutes. If you feel like crying, don't hold back. Crying is good here. If you have inflicted pain on your partner, you *should* feel sad.

■ STEP THREE

For this third step, reposition yourselves so you are both on a 45-degree angle again to your partner and to the mirror. We want you now to raise your hands above your heads. Imagine that the tips of your fingers are positioned on top of your own barriers. Say the following words to yourselves: "I forgive you for hurting me. I forgive myself for responding so negatively to the feelings of abandonment I experienced when you hurt me."

Simultaneously and slowly, lower your hands while imagining that you are both dissolving the barriers that have separated the two of you. When both of your barriers are completely lowered — as evidenced by your hands being lowered into your laps — sit for a minute or two more, looking at each other in the mirror while imagining that there are no barriers to separate you.

■ STEP FOUR

Next, reposition yourselves once again to face each other. This time, though, there should be no space between you. You should be sitting with your legs crossed. Your knees should be touching. Take your partner's hands in yours. Look into each other's eyes and repeat the following words (it doesn't matter who says them first): "I am so sorry that I've hurt you. I promise you that I will never say anything to you or do anything that hurts you. I promise that I will be your best friend forever." Now hold your partner's face gently in your hands and kiss their mouth softly.

■ STEP FIVE

For the final step, once again position yourselves so that you are facing one another. There is no such thing as being too close to one another at this point.

Now imagine that this is the first time you and your partner have met. Remember what that felt like. Hold your partner's hands in your hands. Gaze, once again, into each other's eyes. There is only peacefulness between you. There are no longer any barriers. You both recognize that this first-time meeting is special. And, without speaking the words, you convey to each other that you are both open to being loved.

■ A NEW BEGINNING

You now have an opportunity that most of us are not often granted. You and your partner have a chance to start over from the beginning. You now have the opportunity to maintain a heightened awareness of your best friend every moment of the day. But remember this — the world outside of your home is a very difficult one. It's extremely difficult to make a living; pay all of our expenses on time; raise our children to be healthy, happy, and productive adults; be competent at our jobs every day; get along with our fellow employees; keep ourselves centered; and grow a little bit each day so that we can become the person we always wanted to become. It is a big bad world out there.

You and your partner, though, are in this life together. You must always be on each other's side. It's much easier to go through life with your best friend than alone.

Never let anyone or anything come between the two of you. Never allow your partner to feel that you are not *100 percent* on their side. Cherish your friendship. Be each other's best friend every day. Help them when they need help. Hold them when they need to be held. Understand that each of us has our own struggles, and respect the fact that your partner is doing his or her best. Don't allow even one brick to become the base of a new barrier that your partner begins to build. If you screw up again — and you will from time to time — *recognize* that you've messed up and tell your partner that you're sorry. Kiss them often. Hold them even more often. Only provide positive input. You will be rewarded with ten times what you give.

You will be best friends forever.

PART
SIX

Postscript

CHAPTER 16

WHAT IF IT DOESN'T WORK?

$\mathcal{D}$oes it ever happen that a couple tries, but finds they CAN'T break down barriers? Unfortunately the answer is yes. It's sad when it becomes too late to repair the damage done to a relationship. If you should find yourself in this position, however, it is very important to remember not to compound the loss of your dream by hurting your children or partner further.

Lucy and Mark came into my office together. They had attempted to reconcile their marriage through marriage counseling. It was not successful. Mark was ready to dissolve their marriage. Lucy was not. Lucy came with Mark because, as she put it, she wanted to protect her legal position. She stated, from the very beginning, that she wasn't going to cooperate in the mediation process. She said that if Mark didn't want to be married to her any longer, she would make his life as miserable as she possibly could. She also said that she would eliminate him from their son's life, if she could do so. Mark understood that mediation of the issues wasn't possible, but he wanted our help with attempting to convince Lucy not to keep their child embroiled in conflict through her anger, both during the dissolution process and afterwards.

Since Lucy said she wasn't going to cooperate in the mediation of issues of their dissolution of their marriage, no mediation efforts were attempted. Mark clearly stated that he did not want to reconcile their marriage. Mark did, however, ask if he could explain why he felt that way. He began by explaining that when he and Lucy met, Lucy told him that he had potential, but that he needed some help with lots of things — including (but not limited to) how he dressed, the way he combed his hair, his posture, and how he spoke to and acted around her parents. At first, he said, he thought Lucy's interest in him was great. He liked the attention, and, of course, when he listened she showed her approval. She went with him to purchase clothes and she picked them out. She even picked out what he was to wear when they went out on a date.

Lucy, Mark said, needed to have input about everything. He didn't dress right when she didn't dress him. He didn't know how to do his hair. When he was with her parents, he didn't say the right things or kiss them hello and goodbye. She couldn't understand how he could discuss some of the things he discussed when he was with their friends. Nothing he did seemed good enough. It took a while for him to feel that way, though. For a year or two he listened and behaved. Then, he said, he began to resent the fact that if it wasn't Lucy's way, it wasn't the right way. He felt as though he had to walk carefully, as though he were walking on eggshells.

Mark continued to say that after a while he was certain that Lucy didn't like him the way he was naturally. Nothing could please her. As a matter of fact, Mark said that he would bring Lucy breakfast in bed a few times a week. He'd make her a fried egg or two and bring her toast, orange juice, and coffee — but, if the yoke of the fried egg was broken, Lucy made Mark go back to the kitchen, throw out the egg and make another so the yoke wasn't broken when he brought it to her. Mark said that he tried to explain to Lucy that she was making him feel unwanted and unloved. Lucy told him that his feelings were ridiculous. She said that she was just showing him how much she loved him by trying to help him improve.

When Mark finally — after 10 years of marriage — said that he wanted a divorce because he felt that Lucy just couldn't accept him the way he was and simply didn't like him, Lucy said, "But now I like you." Sadly, Mark said, it was too late.

It was evident that there wasn't much to be done as far as mediating issues of Lucy and Mark's dissolution. But I tried to help by offering them these words: "Lucy and Mark, there is one thing that you must remember as you go through this extremely traumatic time of your life: when your son Aaron was born and you looked at him for the very first time, that the last thing you ever dreamed would happen is that the two of you would do anything that would cause him to grow up to be less healthy than you'd both like him to be. If you keep him embroiled in conflict either during the dissolution process or after it's over, he will feel torn. He will want to be loved by you, Lucy, and by you, Mark; he will want to have approval from both of you and he will want to be loyal to both of you. If you put him in the middle and cause him to feel that he's being pulled by each of you, he will grow up to be less healthy than he could be. Don't do it. Be careful. He's very fragile, too.

Please be careful not to hurt him. Try to give up the anger you feel at each other and at yourselves for whatever role you played in bringing your marriage to this point."

Both Lucy and Mark had tears in their eyes as the session came to a close. Both believed that I was right. Both promised they would try to raise Aaron to be healthy. I remember thinking at the time, "I hope they reflect on this moment as they move through this awful time of their lives."

APPENDIX A

QUICK REFERENCE:

A Man's Guide to Being a Woman's Best Friend

■ BE TOTALLY HONEST ABOUT EVERYTHING, EVEN THE SMALLEST DETAIL

It seems to me that inherent in every woman's nature is her need to know everything about her man. Men are very different from women in that way. Most men are not concerned about with whom she ate lunch, or what she ate for lunch. They don't care what she talked about. Women need to know details. Details are important to a woman.

Not only is it important to tell her every detail if she asks, it's imperative to tell her the *truth* about every detail. If you don't tell her the truth, she'll instinctively know it. Women somehow know when their man is not being entirely honest. She may not *tell* you that she knows you're not telling the truth, but it registers, and she never forgets.

You must remember that always telling her the truth is a critical element of being her best friend. Simply stated, if she senses that you're not telling the truth, she won't feel completely secure and safe. If she doesn't feel completely secure and safe, she'll withhold the really special parts of her that she wants to give you. And if she feels that she has to withhold even part of herself from you, she will not let herself truly be your best friend. She begins to build a barrier between you and her that becomes higher and thicker each time you don't tell her the truth. That barrier may become impossible for you to penetrate.

> *"When someone tells you the truth,*
> *lets you think for yourself,*
> *experience your own emotions,*
> *he is treating you as a true equal.*
> *As a friend."*
> —Whitney Otto

■ LISTEN TO HER WITHOUT INTERRUPTING

If you expect her to want to be your best friend, you must understand that, to her, listening is an important aspect of "foreplay." Uninterrupted eye contact is critical. Asking questions is not. It's helpful, but not necessary, that you pay strict attention to every word she says. She'll know that your mind is wandering after she's taken seven or eight minutes to tell you everything about the life of the clerk at the market. She'll also know, however, that you've listened, you didn't interrupt, and you were patient. If you don't listen to her without interrupting, she will never feel completely comfortable being able to share her thoughts and feelings with you.

■ CUDDLE WITH HER IN THE MORNING AND BRING HER COFFEE

Cuddling with her in the morning and bringing her coffee is not on the level of importance as telling the truth about everything, or listening to her. However, it reminds her that, first thing each day, you think about her comfort level.

We all hear that woman love to cuddle and men don't. We don't know how that belief got started. It's not about sex, it's about starting each day with a moment or two of peacefulness and closeness. When you do cuddle with her in the morning, you may find that you'll hear yourself whimper slightly, as you rest your knees closely behind hers, and put your arm around her arm. The feeling is that nice. She'll know that you are letting yourself be open and vulnerable, as she starts her day feeling secure in the knowledge that you are the love of her life.

■ TELL HER TO BE SAFE AS YOU KISS HER GOODBYE IN THE MORNING

This is another way of saying "I love you." It tells her that you cherish sharing your life with her, and that you understand how dangerous our world has become. It tells her that you want her to pay attention to everything going on around her, so that you're safely back together again that evening.

"Kind words can be short and easy to speak
but their echoes are truly endless."
— Mother Theresa

■ SHOWER AND SHAVE BEFORE GETTING INTO BED AT NIGHT AND THEN DON'T BOTHER HER

We know that you're exhausted at the end of each day. We're all exhausted at the end of the day. We're not suggesting that you actually take a shower and shave *every* night before you get into bed to go to sleep. But get a full-sized picture of this. She's in bed watching television. She hears you in the bathroom with the faucet running, and then she hears you turn on the shower. She's thinking, "Does he really expect me to make love to him tonight?" You finish, and get into bed. A few minutes later, you roll over, kiss her gently, and say "I love you, honey — sleep well." Guess what she's thinking. No, it's not "What's wrong with him." It's "Good boy." She smiles to herself, cuddles down and, as she drifts off to sleep, thinks "Now *that* man is my friend."

■ GO GROCERY SHOPPING WITH HER ON FRIDAY NIGHT AND HELP PUT THE GROCERIES AWAY

Assuming she works outside the house daily, you must realize that she is truly carrying two full-time jobs. She is probably primarily responsible for making sure the house is clean, the kids are cared for, you and they are fed, and your clothes are clean. She tries to be sure that she's well groomed and as pretty as possible. Sound overwhelming? It is. So, the work week is finally over, and, being aware that the refrigerator is empty, she says, "I need to go grocery shopping." What do you do? (1) You watch the basketball game while she goes shopping. (2) You tell her that you have work and ask her to buy a 6-pack of beer. (3) You tell her that you want to go out with your friends. (4) You go grocery shopping with her, kiss her in front of the produce section, and then help put the groceries away when you get home. If you haven't picked (4), look for her to eventually be fantasizing about the guy she regularly sees at the market. Get the message?

■ NEVER SAY ANYTHING THAT WILL CAUSE HER TO FEEL UNWORTHY

We are all sensitive to negative input, especially from someone we love. Anytime you say things like "You're lazy" or "You can't cook," she will shut down emotionally in order to protect herself from being hurt by you again. Verbal abuse is as devastating as physical abuse. If you say things that cause her to feel unworthy, she might go through the motions of being with you — perhaps even for years — but you've hurt her, you've not been her friend, and it may be very difficult to regain her trust.

"No one can make you feel inferior without your consent."
— Eleanor Roosevelt

■ NEVER SAY ANYTHING THAT WILL EMBARRASS HER

Women — much more so than men — are very sensitive to words used to describe them. Especially when you are with friends or family, anything you say about her that makes her feel self-conscious will embarrass her, even if you were attempting to be funny or cute. You may think that saying something that embarrasses her is insignificant. You may even attempt to brush it off, and say something like, "You're being too sensitive; no one thought anything about it." To her, though, it's not insignificant. It's a major breach of trust. It's a major breach of friendship. She'll never forget that you were thoughtless and, although other things you may do or say to her over the years may be more hurtful, she will remember that you betrayed her. To her, it is a form of abandonment.

"Friendship is a sheltering tree."
— Samuel Taylor Coleridge, *Youth and Age*

■ NEVER GO INTO HER PURSE FOR ANYTHING

To a woman, her purse is as personal as her diary. It is that place where she stores highly personal things and information that she carries with her daily. It's the place where she keeps the secrets of how she maintains her youthfulness and beauty. It's the place where she hides those few extra dollars she is saving for something important she needs. It's her portable desk. It's hers, not yours. There is no excuse for violating her privacy. If you need to get something that you know is in her purse, bring it to her so she can retrieve it herself. It's a way of showing her that you respect her privacy. It's another way of showing her that she can feel safe in your presence.

> *"Wouldn't it be nice if everybody understood without*
> *being told that you need a certain amount of space?"*
> — Mary Higgins Clark

■ DON'T DOMINATE CONVERSATION ABOUT YOUR WORK

There is no denying that money you earn from your work is necessary to providing the essentials of life to those you love, but you don't have to talk about your work every day. Dominating conversation about your work is ego-centric. To her, it may seem as though you don't feel that anything she is doing has significance. It detracts from the brief moments during your day when you and she can share a laugh, a story about someone you know, a moment to discuss the news events of the day, or a moment of quiet and peacefulness at home.

> *"Let there be spaces in your togetherness."*
> — Kahlil Gibran, *The Prophet. On Marriage*

■ GIVE UP ANGER YOU HAVE AT YOURSELF

There are things that each of us have done during our lifetime of which we are ashamed. Many of us, too, have not lived up to either our own expectations, or the expectations that others have had for us. Some of us have been either physically or emotionally abusive to someone for whom we have expressed feelings of love.

It will be difficult for you to be sensitive to her needs, express your deepest feelings of love and devotion, and be open and honest about yourself if you don't give up the anger you have at yourself. You might consider looking at it this way: Assume for a moment that you had a childhood boyfriend who you loved and adored, but, for some reason, you said or did something that deeply hurt that friend. Your friend told you that he did not want you to be a part of his life. After a month or two of missing your friend, you approached him, said that you were sincerely sorry, and asked for his forgiveness. Of course, your boyhood friend forgave you, and you continued to have this dear friend in your life.

If you are to be your own best friend — and no one can be your best friend better — then you must forgive yourself for all of those things in your lifetime of which you are ashamed. You must do this if you hope to become *her* best friend, because the anger that you harbor at yourself may, on occasion, be projected at her, and you can't let that happen.

> *"Were it offered to my choice, I should have no objections*
> *to a repetition of the same life from its beginning,*
> *only asking the advantages authors have in a second*
> *edition to correct some faults of the first."*
> — Benjamin Franklin

■ ALWAYS DO YOUR BEST AT YOUR JOB

When you asked for her love, inherent in that promise was the promise that you would always try to be responsible and conscientious about everything in your life. Whether or not that promise was verbalized or implied, you expressed your intent to work hard to provide a nice standard of living for her and your family. One way to keep that promise is to always do your best at your job.

■ ESTABLISH AND LIVE WITHIN YOUR BUDGET

Neither you nor she can be at peace with yourselves or one another if together you spend more money than your income permits. Everything in your life together may be wonderful. You may be achieving the highest level of success at being her best friend. You will not be able, however, to eliminate as many levels of her anxiety as you would like to eliminate unless you successfully live within a responsibly established budget that the two of you establish together.

If you are unable to meet your financial responsibilities, seek help *together* from a consumer credit counseling organization or a financial advisor, and *together* make those difficult decisions that most of us, at some time in our life, must make. Include her in all of those decisions, so that she also understands that, unless your financial state of affairs is well balanced, the two of you will not be able to connect as freely and comfortably as you would like.

"Life is like a blanket too short.
You pull it up and your toes rebel, you yank it down
and shivers meander about your shoulder;
but cheerful folks manage to draw their knees up
and pass a very comfortable night."
— Marion Howard

■ NEVER DO ANYTHING THAT IS EMBARRASSING

The manner in which you conduct your life is a reflection on her. If you become angry in public at someone who is providing a service to you, it is a reflection on her. If you are responsible for being late for appointments or to pick up friends, it is a reflection on her. If you drink or abuse alcohol or drugs, it is a reflection on her. When you do things that are embarrassing to yourself, she is embarrassed not only for you but for herself.

"I have to live with my own truth.
I have to live with it.
You live with your own truth.
I cannot live with it."
— Maria Irene Fornes

■ GIVE HER SPACE WHEN SHE NEEDS IT

Every woman needs her privacy. It's sufficient that she tolerates your presence when she first wakes up each morning, looking like she's not sure what to herself. It's enough that either you or the children are clamoring for her attention all day, in one way or another. When she needs to be alone to put on her makeup, dry off from her shower, or read a book, respect her need for privacy. If you do, she'll feel better about sharing more time with you.

"You love me so much, you want to put me in your pocket.
And I should die there smothered."
— D.H. Lawrence

■ ALWAYS MAKE EYE CONTACT WHEN SHE IS SPEAKING TO YOU OR YOU TO HER

When you are speaking to her or she is speaking to you, the message contained in the words is not as important to her as the personal contact between the two of you. She listens to your words with her eyes; even more so than with her ears. When your eye contact waivers, her ability to hear you declines. Similarly, she feels that you are not paying attention to her if you are not making eye contact. It's one of the reasons you may hear her say "You never listen to anything I say."

She may begin to feel abandoned by you for one of many reasons. For example, she may feel abandoned when she is feeling a little low and you are not sensitive and attentive to her. By and of itself, your lack of consistent eye contact doesn't send the signal to her that she needs to be afraid that you will abandon her, but the problem becomes compounded if you spend too much time with your friends, working, or watching sports on television. It's a part of her perception of how you feel about her. You must be careful not to give her reason to be afraid. If she has even a small level of anxiety, she will not be open and comfortable when she is with you, so be sure your eye contact is always good.

"The eyes, those silent tongues of Love."
— Cervantes

■ TAKE OUT THE GARBAGE

Even though women are rapidly proving to themselves and to the world that they are as bright or brighter, as competitive or more competitive, and as capable of completing any task with every bit as high a level of competence as any man, women respect men. In particular, women respect a man who is a gentleman.

You are probably physically stronger than she is. You probably don't mind picking a dead bug off of the floor, even though she is a little squeamish about it. Be a "man," take out the garbage. She'll quietly appreciate you doing this for her and, if you do, she'll probably continue to wash your underwear for you.

> *"Love sought is good,*
> *but giv'n unsought is better."*
> — Shakespeare, *Twelfth Night, Act III*

■ TAKE HER OUT WHEN SHE HASN'T HAD TIME TO PREPARE DINNER

Most likely she considers herself to be responsible for preparing dinner each evening, although she may work outside the home in a full-time job. You might consider assuming equal responsibility for preparing dinner yourself, if you haven't previously done so. When you do this you'll understand how time-consuming — to say nothing of mind-consuming — this responsibility can be. You want dinner to be nutritious and well balanced. You want variety. You want it to be creative and look and taste good. You want it to be prepared on time. After you've assumed this responsibility at least three nights per week, you'll understand why taking her out when she hasn't had time to prepare dinner is more of a gesture of showing that you love her than bringing her a dozen red roses.

> *"My man of men."*
> — Shakespeare, *Anthony and Cleopatra, Act I*

■ NEVER EXPECT ANYTHING IN RETURN

If you are being her best friend, you won't have time to think about what she will give you in return. She will be giving you *so* much, you will be overwhelmed by the feeling of being so loved.

> *"Here are fruits, flowers, leaves and branches,*
> *and here is my heart which beats only for you."*
> — Paul Verlaine, *Romances sans Paroles*

■ SOMETIMES HOLD HER FACE IN YOUR HANDS AS YOU KISS HER MOUTH GENTLY

She loves when you are tender. She loves you when are sensuous. She loves you when you hold her face gently in your hands and kiss her mouth ever so sweetly. She is your love, and *only* your love, and it will be you about whom she will fantasize during her busy day.

> *"The kiss you take is better than you give."*
> — Shakespeare, *Troilus and Cressida*, Act IV

■ NEVER PATRONIZE HER

Always remember that her work is as important as your work. Her thoughts are as profound as your thoughts. Her ideas are as great as your ideas; and her intelligence level is equally as high — or higher — than yours. If you say anything to her that implies you feel differently, she will lose respect for you.

> *"Whether women are better than men I cannot say —*
> *but I can say they are certainly no worse."*
> — Golda Meir

■ **BRING HER BREAKFAST IN BED ONCE IN A WHILE**

You don't need to be earning "big bucks" in order to shower her with lavish gifts. Bring her breakfast in bed once in a while; she'll feel like a princess. She will smile and laugh a little, and she will say "Why are you doing this?" It's not necessary to answer, though, because in her heart she knows it's because you want to see her smile.

> *"Every man feels instinctively*
> *that all the beautiful sentiments in the world*
> *weigh less than a single lovely action."*
> — James Russell Lowell, *Literary Essays, Vol. II*

■ **GIVE HER YOUR JACKET WHEN SHE FEELS COLD**

If she has to tell you when she's feeling cold, you are not being as observant as you need to be. How often have you thought, to yourself or out loud, "Am I supposed to be able to read your mind?" The answer is no, but you *should* be able to anticipate her needs. You can see if she's tired or slightly irritable. You can see if she's feeling happy or sad. You can see if she's pre-occupied or able to devote her attention to you. You can certainly see if she's cold. There isn't anything you can do for her that is sexier than being able to anticipate her needs. Try it. She'll know that although you can't read her mind, you are definitely tuned into it.

> *"Oh, my Luve is like a red, red rose,*
> *That's newly sprung in June.*
> *O, my Luve is like the melodie,*
> *That's sweetly played in tune."*
> — Robert Burns, *A Red, Red Rose*

■ HAVE HER CAR WASHED AND FILLED WITH GAS OVER THE WEEKEND

You know how you feel when you get into a car that has been freshly washed, vacuumed, scented, and filled with gas. If for only an instant, you feel like your life is slightly more orderly, and you know that you don't have to stand in the freezing cold or heat of the summer to fill your car with gas. She feels the same way you do. It takes only a half an hour, and it only requires a small amount of your attention. It subtly conveys the message that you are dedicated to making her life as comfortable as possible.

"You roll my log, and I will roll yours."
— Seneca, *Apocolocyntosis, Sec. 9*

■ IF SHE'S EMPLOYED, LET HER KNOW THAT YOU APPRECIATE THAT SHE'S REALLY CARRYING TWO FULL-TIME JOBS

There are ways to let her know that you appreciate that she is really carrying two full-time jobs. Say thank you when she prepares dinner. Take out the garbage. Prepare the children's school lunches. Help her clean the house. Empty the dishwasher. Clean the bathroom sink and wipe the water spots off the mirror. Pick your clothes up off of the floor. Replace the empty roll of toilet paper. Clear the table after dinner.

If you do anything less, she will think that you are oblivious to the amount of work with which she copes every day. She will become angry that you are not helping her; she will tell you how she's feeling. If you have a tendency to be defensive when she says, "Can't you help a little?," get over it. If you want to be her best friend, help her. If you don't care if you lose her, then don't.

"Now join your hands,
and with your hands your hearts."
— Shakespeare, *King Henry the Sixth, Part III, Act IV*

■ MAKE LOVE TO HER

In actuality, every section in this book explains how you can "make love" to her. Making love does not begin when the two of you decide to make love. It starts from the moment you and she awake each morning and ends when you close your eyes as you fall asleep at night. As we explained earlier, foreplay begins when you show her that you care enough to listen — even though you may know exactly what she is going to say — and continues into the evening when you turn the basketball game off because she sends your daughter to you to watch her practice for her ballet recital.

You make love to her in bed by caring whether she's been satisfied before you. The problem is, if you have made love to her during the day, too, she will want to show you how much she appreciates the many ways you make love to her. She'll want to make love to you much more than you can physically handle. Consequently, when you're not in bed, she will begin making love to you in the same or even more creative ways than you make love to her. (Some problem, huh?)

> *"None shall part us from each other,*
> *One in life and death are we:*
> *All in all to one another —*
> *I to thee and thou to me!*
> *Thou the tree and I the flower—*
> *Thou the idol; I the throng—*
> *Thou the day and I the hour—*
> *Thou the singer; I the song!"*
> — Gilbert

■ BE CONSISTENT IN YOUR BEHAVIOR AND TEMPERAMENT

If she has to worry about how you will react to something she does, because you tend to react differently each time, she will feel anxious when she's with you. She may perceive your inconsistency as controling. It may seem to her that being in your presence causes her to feel like she's always walking on eggshells. She has to be very careful.

If you truly want to be her friend, don't cause her to have to feel this way. Be consistent in your behavior and temperament by being accepting. Let her know not only through your words, but also through your actions, that she doesn't have to fear — even occasionally — an outburst of anger. She'll smile more easily. She'll be more peaceful. She'll thank you by being your best friend.

> *"Friendship has too much resembled for men*
> *the camaraderie of battle,*
> *for women the consolations of passivity;*
> *marriage has owed too much to romance,*
> *too little to friendship."*
> — Carolyn G. Heilbrun

■ DON'T RUSH HER BEFORE THE TWO OF YOU ARE LEAVING TO GO SOMEWHERE

If men are from Mars and women are from Venus, then the pace on Mars is much faster than on Venus. It simply takes a woman longer to get ready to leave the house than it takes a man. Find something to do. Find anything to do. Read the newspaper, put loose change in wrappers, play solitaire, or organize your schedule for the next day. Do anything, but don't get into the car and start the engine before she is absolutely ready to walk out the door.

"The key to everything is patience.
You get the chicken by hatching the egg —
not by smashing it."
— Arnold Glasow

■ KNOW WHEN HER MENSTRUAL CYCLE BEGINS AND DON'T EXPECT TO BE PATTED ON THE BACK JUST BECAUSE YOU KNOW THIS

The knowledge most men have of a woman's menstrual cycle is limited to the fact that once every month she becomes bloated, irritable, and shuns intercourse. Most men don't understand the effect a woman's menstrual cycle has on her physical or emotional being. They don't know why she experiences a menstrual cycle and they can't even spell "menstrual." They just don't like it. For those men, here's a news flash: *She* likes it a lot less then you do.

Okay, you don't have to learn to spell menstrual, but it would be helpful to know when her cycle begins so that it's not necessary to say to her every month "What's the matter, getting your period?" You need to understand that these words don't endear you to her. Be sensitive and in touch with her during the days prior to the beginning of her cycle, too. Simply place an "x" on your calendar around the date you expect her cycle to begin, and be more patient, understanding, and helpful.

■ DON'T EVER CRITICIZE HER

It's important you realize that, even if she's lived a charmed existence, most likely there are some people in her life that have been critical of her. Equally as important, she is critical of herself. She doesn't need to be told by you when she screws up, or when her hair or make-up isn't perfect. She doesn't need to be told by you that dinner wasn't just the way you like it. She doesn't need to be told that your children's behavior is unacceptable and she should do something about it.

Best friends are not critical of each other. They accept any negative attributes along with all the positive attributes. Of all the people in the world, she expects you to unconditionally love and accept her. If you accept anything you may perceive as somewhat negative and don't even mildly suggest it's negative, you will have done a good thing for yourself.

■ ENCOURAGE HER TO FANTASIZE

It's true that we have our weekends and sometimes we go on vacation, but most of us have to attend to the serious business of life every day.

If you want to be her best friend, encourage her to fantasize. Her fantasies are her little vacations from the drudgery of her everyday life. Her fantasies help to replace the vacations you are unable to take as often as you'd like. Her fantasies help to make her more playful when she's with you. She will fantasize anyway. You may as well understand and accept that fact so she won't find a need to transform her fantasies into a real-life adventure.

■ DON'T SMOKE OR ABUSE ALCOHOL AND DRUGS

Women are attracted to men who are clean, well groomed, and smell good. Women are attracted to men who are in touch with themselves and others.

Smoking is a smelly, dirty habit that can kill not only you but also people around you. If you are smoking, she believes that you not only don't care about your *own* health, but also you don't care about her health or the health of your children. She believes you may die younger than you should, she's tired of hearing that you are going to stop smoking soon, and she doesn't like the way you smell.

If you are abusing alcohol and drugs, your behavior is not reminiscent of the behavior of the man she married, or the man she hoped you would someday become. Alcohol and drugs obliterate your senses. They cloud your perception of reality. They don't allow you to be in touch with yourself or her. If you are abusing alcohol or drugs, the time you have left to be with her may be limited.

■ NEVER LET HER SEE YOU LOOKING AT ANOTHER WOMAN

Ideally, each woman would like to be able to look in the mirror and think to herself, "Hello, gorgeous." Realistically, there probably isn't a woman in the world — including those few that are movie stars and models — who have that thought. Most women are extremely critical of how they look. Most women wish their hair had a better sheen, their face didn't have a blemish, or that their nose and butt were shaped differently.

She wants to look better not only because she wants to look good for you, but because she compares herself to other women. These comparisons are not at her first level of consciousness; they're just always lurking somewhere below that level — except when her peripheral vision allows her to see your eyes darting quickly in the direction of another woman. Believe me, she has great peripheral vision. When it comes to noticing whether you are looking at another woman, she sees everything. It's not a jealousy thing, either — don't get that idea.

She also wants you to find her attractive and sexy. Anything you can do or say that lets her feel that you think she is magnificent to be with, do or say. You should help to prevent her from feeling, if even for a fleeting moment, that you find another woman sexy. So just don't let her see you looking at another woman. It's not good for either of you, and if she feels that you think she is attractive and sexy, she will be much more attractive and sexy than either you or she ever imagined she could be.

> *"A courteous person will always make everyone around him*
> *feel at his best and most alive." He will bring to his meeting*
> *with another person an absolutely genuine interest, respect and*
> *concern for that person; and above all, he will give him his whole*
> *attention without curiosity or demand, and so immediately*
> *communicate to the other a freedom and sureness*
> *of which, perhaps, he did not know himself to be capable."*
> — Helen M. Luke

■ BE HER PLAYMATE

From time to time, glance deeply and carefully into her eyes. If you are being her friend in the sense we are describing, you will almost always see a twinkle just ready and waiting to come out and play. Allow your twinkle to play with her twinkle, and you'll find that the two of you will be making love without being in bed, and smiling at each other much more.

> *"...wit...is, after all, a form of arousal.*
> *We challenge one another to be funnier and smarter.*
> *It's high-energy play.*
> *It's the way friends make love to one another."*
> — Anne Gottlieb

■ MAINTAIN A LIFE INSURANCE POLICY ON YOURSELF

Reality check! Any of us could die tomorrow. If you love her, you must be protective of her in life as well as in death. Although none of us consciously think about death, subconsciously it hovers over us. You can help her to feel more secure, and relieve her of yet another level of anxiety, if you maintain a life insurance policy on yourself. Don't leave this stone unturned.

■ HELP HER TO EXAMINE HER BREASTS AND ENCOURAGE HER TO GET A MAMMOGRAM AND PHYSICAL EXAMINATION EVERY YEAR

Now this you should do every day. Perhaps even twice a day. Seriously, although it is extremely uncomfortable for her to have a mammogram, it's imperative that she examine her breasts often. It's an absolute necessity for her to not only get a mammogram but also a physical examination every year. You must have a physical examination every year too if you really are going to be her best friend. Tell her that you always want her to be healthy and with you. Encourage her to make an appointment to see her doctor.

■ SHOWER AND SHAVE BEFORE YOU MAKE LOVE TO HER

Imagine for a moment that you were getting ready to take her out on a date early in your relationship. That you're really attracted to her. You're comfortable with her, and you sense she might be ready to make love to you. You would, of course, shower and shave and be sure your nails and hair were clean and well groomed. You would want her to think to herself, "He smells so good." She becomes aroused more easily when you are clean and your face feels soft against her skin.

Our lives are filled with so many things on which we must concentrate each day, that it's naturally difficult for each of us to transfer the focus of our attention away from our very busy schedules. You shouldn't expect that after she has worked all day, picked up the children, made dinner for you all, washed, dried and folded the laundry, and put the children to bed, that it will be easy for her to refocus her attention on your (or her) sexual needs. She's exhausted. She probably just wants to take her make-up off, have a bath, read a book or watch television, and fall off to a good night's sleep.

On the other hand, making love is a terrific way to erase the tension of the day, share a wonderfully intimate experience, and help get you both off to a peaceful sleep. Take a shower and shave before you get into bed, smile softly at her as if to ask, "Do I have to be your friend tonight and let you go to sleep?" She'll be more ready to make love to you than she would be if you hadn't taken the time to be clean and soft for her.

"He is every other inch a gentleman."
— Dame Rebecca West

■ ENJOY AND APPRECIATE THE LITTLE GIRL IN HER

Every woman has, tucked away somewhere in a special little place inside of her, vivid memories of herself as a little girl. She smiles to herself when she remembers how she pretended she was her doll's teacher, how she dressed up in her mom's high heels as she pretended she was going out to dinner with her husband, and how she watched out the front window of her house just get a glimpse of that boy she thought was *sooo* cute. From time to time, if you watch her carefully out of the corner of your eye, you'll recognize a special look or certain way she'll smile when something happens that causes her to recall one of those memories. It's then you'll see the little girl in her.

You can be her boyfriend, her husband, or her lover, but you can't be her best friend unless she allows you to share that special place with you. She will only share it if she unequivocally trusts you. She will only share it if you are able to recognize it without her pointing it out to you. She may have never shared it with any one else in her life. She'd love to share it with you. She wants you to see it, but she wants you to find it yourself.

> *"We are all the same people as we were*
> *at three, six, ten or twenty years old.*
> *More noticeably so, perhaps, at six or seven,*
> *because we were not pretending so much then."*
> —Agatha Christie

■ BRING HER WATER AND SOMETHING FOR HER HEADACHE

You can relax a little bit with this one, guys. There's no need for you to raise the level of your insightfulness here. Think about it this way: if you and she are best friends, she is doing things for you and you for her just because you're buddies. You hang out and go places together, she's on your side and you're on hers all the time. You hear her say, "I've got a terrible headache." Bring her water and something for her headache. Don't make her get it herself. It's no big deal. But it's another little thing that conveys the message that she needs to hear.

■ KEEP EVERY PROMISE

From the very first moment you and she met, you began making promises to her. The following is a partial list of things you did for her or how you behaved when you were with her and the promise that you implicitly made to her as a result of those actions or behavior. Most of your promises were never verbalized. They were implied by your actions or behavior.

The way you were	Your Promise
You were well groomed.	You promised to always be well groomed and clean.
You were polite.	You promised to always be polite.
You were on time for a date.	You promised to always be on time.
You were considerate of her.	You promised to always be considerate.
You didn't yell at her.	You promised never to yell at her.
You worked hard at your job.	You promised to always work hard at your job.
You never embarrassed her.	You promised never to embarrass her.
You listened to her opinion.	You promised to always listen to her opinion.
You were trustworthy.	You promised to always be trustworthy.

In addition to your non-verbalized promises, there are promises that you verbalize. When you say "I'll be home at 6," or "I'll make a deposit today," you are asking her to rely upon you to be home at 6 or make that deposit. To her, these promises are not trivial. It's a mistake for you to consider them to be trivial. The feeling of trust you want her to have in you is reduced each time you break either a verbalized or non-verbalized promise. She can't trust you if you break promises to her. Her trust can only be earned if you consistently, over a very long period of time, don't break promises.

■ NEVER MAKE A LEFT-HAND TURN WITH HER IN THE PASSENGER SEAT UNLESS YOU ARE ABSOLUTELY CERTAIN THERE'S NO RISK FROM ONCOMING TRAFFIC

Suppose for just a moment that you are driving your car and she is in the passenger seat. The traffic is a little congested and you find yourself having to wait longer than normal to make a left-hand turn. Suddenly, you see that opening you've been waiting for, but you realize that you have to accelerate quickly to make your turn. So you push the peddle to the floor, the car lurches forward and as it does you realize the car bearing down on you is traveling at a faster speed than the other cars. You successfully make your turn, however, with a couple of seconds to spare.

For your edification, here's her thought process. When you move to the left-hand lane to make that turn, she is thinking "The traffic is moving really fast." While you're waiting longer than normal for the opening to occur in traffic, she is thinking "I hope he realizes that I'm on the side of the car that gets hit first." When she feels you accelerate and the car lurches forward, her stomach drops, her heartbeat quickens, and she sees the car in the oncoming traffic lane that is traveling faster than the other cars, coming directly at her door. She is thinking, "I hope the car doesn't stall or his foot doesn't slip off the accelerator. Oh God, I hope we make it."

Fortunately, you did successfully negotiate the turn, and you say something she doesn't think is very cute, like "We had enough time to make that turn twice." She is thinking "What a jerk. Isn't he concerned about my safety in the least?" She may or may not say something to you at that moment. But consciously or subconsciously she remembers that you did something really stupid that placed her life in danger. You didn't care about how fearful she felt when that oncoming car was bearing down on her. She's thinking "He really doesn't care about me."

If you really want to be her best friend, you should help to reduce anxiety in her life, not to create more. Don't do it again, or she'll soon be verbalizing what she *was* thinking which was "You don't really care about me."

■ SCRATCH HER BACK IN THE MORNING

While you're cuddling with her in the morning, just before you bring her coffee, scratch her back for a few minutes. It feels wonderful to her, especially because she's just awoken from a sound sleep. It's another way to let her know she's loved.

■ BE PATIENT WITH YOUR CHILDREN

Being patient with your children is an indication to her that you are under control. Provided she thinks that you are feeling calm, she can concentrate on herself and the dozens of things on which she must concentrate. When you're patient with your children, she will be inclined to think that you will be patient with her. It will help her to feel more peaceful.

Being patient with your children also lets her know that you are contributing to raising them to become healthy, productive adults. She won't feel she is the only one responsible for raising them. By being patient you also fulfill one of the most important qualities she hoped you'd have when she was considering being with you. That you'd help her to raise your children to feel good about themselves by constantly conveying positive feelings to them. Each time you are patient with your children, you're saying to her "Be calm, honey, we're all doing fine." There is no better gift you can give her.

"The fault no child ever loses
is the one he was most punished for."
— Cesare Beccaria

■ CALL HER WHENEVER YOU'RE GOING TO BE LATER THAN SHE EXPECTS

She is expecting you to be home for dinner at 6 p.m. You normally are home at around that time, but on this day your 4:30 meeting took longer than you expected. It's now 5:45 and you finish your meeting, return a phone call or two, and make some notes for the following day.

She knows you're hungry when you get home each day, so she starts dinner at 5:30. It's now 6 and she tells the kids to wash up for dinner. She listens for your car to pull into the driveway, so she can begin to tie all the elements of her meal together. She hopes you're going to like what she's prepared.

You leave the office and the traffic is still heavy. It's now 6:20 and you realize you're not going to be home until 6:45. The kids are starting to complain that they're hungry. She is concerned that her dinner is overcooked, and those things she's removed from the oven are getting cold. You're not late too often, so she's beginning to wonder if you are okay.

You walk into your home at 6:45 and she says, "Where were you?" You explain what happened and she says "Sit down and eat your dinner." You can't understand why she's angry. Simply, you didn't separate yourself from your involvement of your workday at 6, when you needed to be picturing what was going on at home. You must be able to tune in to her and everything going on in your home all the time. You must remember that there is never a good excuse for being inconsiderate. Saying you're sorry just doesn't cut it.

> *"How is it that so often... I get the feeling I've worked*
> *hard to learn something I already know, or knew, once."*
> — Linda Ellerbee

■ DON'T BRING YOUR WORK HOME TOO OFTEN

For those of you who think that you are fulfilling her need to feel loved by working 10 to 14 hours per day, you couldn't be more wrong. It goes without saying that each of us must provide a home and food for our family. It's really good if you earn enough money to be able to provide a lovely home, a nice car, and a vacation now and then. Being conscientious and working hard at your job is an element of being her best friend. It's taken for granted that you must work to provide for your family, just as you must breathe to remain alive.

But when you bring your work home too often, you may be neglecting her needs. She may begin to feel that your career is your first priority. You might hear her say "All you do is work." What she really means is "I'm feeling neglected." If you bring your work home too often, and if you are not being her best friend in the many other ways discussed in this book, she may feel that you have abandoned her. If she feels that way, she may abandon *you* emotionally. Finally, if she hasn't been able to help you understand that you are neglecting the important aspects of your relationship, she may leave you. It'll be a rude awakening, and it will be too late.

> *"Money often costs too much."*
> — Ralph Waldo Emerson

■ NEVER COMPARE HER TO ANY OTHER WOMAN

We don't think it's necessary to tell you that you shouldn't say something like "Why can't you wear your hair like your friend Carol K.?" or "The way Noreen W. puts on her make-up makes her look younger than you." If you have, in the past, said things like that to her, she already thinks you're so clueless, and it's probably too late to help you. Let's presume, however, that you haven't been that blatant in your comparisons. She may feel you are comparing her to other women when:

- You look at the nude or semi-nude pictures in *Playboy* magazine.
- You look at other women when you're with her.
- You make any positive comment about the appearance of another woman.
- You talk, in a positive way, about a woman with whom you work.
- You ask her why she doesn't read more.
- You ask her why she doesn't take more time to educate herself.
- You comment on the good behavior of another woman's child.

Women are sensitive to, and in touch with, everything going on around them. Their level of sensitivity increases dramatically when it comes to you. It becomes increasingly heightened when you convey the impression that you are paying attention to another woman. She's not jealous. To her, it's a matter of loyalty. You must constantly be aware of her level of sensitivity, and don't do or say anything which even mildly implies that you are comparing her to other women.

> *"An appeaser is one who feeds a crocodile —*
> *hoping it will eat him last."*
> — Winston Churchill

■ NEVER CRITICIZE THE CLOTHES SHE'S WEARING

Unless you are making enough money to allow her to buy her clothes at places like Neiman Marcus, Saks, or Nordstrom's without using any of the money she earns, it's not a good idea to criticize the clothes she's wearing. If you do, and she's as bright, quick, strong and competitive as are most women, her response won't be gentle. So unless you're a masochist, be your own best friend; comment on the weather or what a nice day it is, but don't criticize the clothes she's wearing.

■ SHARE THE RESPONSIBILITY OF DRIVING THE CHILDREN

When you have children, it's "Mom, I have soccer practice," "Mom, I have to go to the library." It's one endless list of places they have to go immediately. Kids will invariably ask their mom to drive them. It's easy for you to continue watching television while pretending you didn't hear your child. It's easy to look like you're preoccupied reading the newspaper. Your feigning being busy may not seem like an obvious omission, and most of the time she'll just do what's asked of her without thinking, "Why couldn't *he* drive her this time?"

When you're married, though, there are no responsibilities that are solely hers or yours. When something needs to be done, it should be done by the one who's most available or the one who's least tired. If the dishes need to be washed and you're available, wash the dishes. If the bed needs to be made, make the bed. If you want her to be your best friend in the true sense of the word, be her friend, too. Just do stuff when it needs to be done; don't wait for her to ask you.

■ ADMIT YOU'VE BEEN WRONG

Since time began, men dominated women. Today, that's not true. Hopefully, you don't feel or act superior to her. One way to let her know you don't feel superior is to readily admit you've been wrong. She'll appreciate that you're open and accept responsibility for your mistakes. She'll appreciate your lack of defensiveness, and that you're not trying to overpower her. Besides, what's the big deal? We all make mistakes sometimes. Just admit you've been wrong. She'll make you feel you were right for doing so.

> *"The road to personal freedom*
> *is paved with responsibility....*
> *The first thing you have to do*
> *is admit the truth and learn from it."*
> — David Viscott

■ NEVER EXPECT HER TO ADMIT SHE IS WRONG

Although today men don't dominate women, most women are still afraid that a man will try to do so. She is always on the lookout for signs that you are starting to be controlling. The worst thing you can do is to make her beg for forgiveness if she makes a mistake. We all make mistakes. (Yes, even men!) When *she's* made one, there is no need to tell her about it. She knows she's made it, and is probably more angry at herself for it than you could ever be. So don't mention it. She'll be able to maintain a peaceful feeling in your presence.

■ NEVER COMMENT ON THE EXISTENCE OF A PIMPLE

If you don't think she knows when she has a pimple, you're really mistaken. A woman checks her face for every blemish, liver spot, wrinkle, and even smile lines. Every woman pays very strict attention to her face. It doesn't matter how tactfully you point out a blemish — if you do, she thinks you're an idiot for doing so. She also thinks that you're insensitive and not focusing on her entire being. If you just have to say something to her because for some reason words just have to come out of your mouth at that moment, say, "Thank you for allowing me to be with you," and kiss her. (But try not to kiss her on the pimple, okay?)

■ HUG HER A COUPLE OF TIMES A DAY

If hugging her a couple of times a day is not in your repertoire, it might be a good idea to start including it. About the second time you do it, she'll say something like, "What are you doing?" She'll pretend like you're annoying her. She may even *feel* like you're annoying her. But she'll love that you want to hug her and need to do it.

■ BE PLEASED WITH ANYTHING SHE'S PREPARED FOR DINNER

Remember, whatever she's prepared for dinner, it was either what she thought you'd like, what she had time to prepare, or what she had the ingredients to prepare. Whatever she prepared, it was the best she could do at that moment. You can be absolutely sure that she wanted to please you, unless you haven't been her best friend up until now. And, oh yes — you're not the one who took the time to prepare dinner. When she brings a baked potato, some cottage cheese, and a salad to the table for your dinner next time, be smart. Say something like, "That was exactly what I've been thinking about all day for dinner. Thank you." There's one more thing, too. Show her how much you appreciate the fact that she made dinner for you. Do the dishes.

■ LET HER KNOW YOU NOTICE AND APPRECIATE EVEN THE SMALLEST THINGS SHE DOES FOR YOU

There are hundreds of things your best friend will do for you — not the least of which is washing your underwear and dirty smelly socks. She'll just do stuff because she thinks it's her job to do them — and because she wants to please you. Make sure you let her know that you notice those things she does. Do little things for her, too. It's the way this whole thing works, you know.

■ ANTICIPATE HER NEEDS

First, make a mental list of all the things you know about your best friend. For example, you know that she wants you to love, respect, and admire her. You know she has grown up in a society that has led her to believe that it's her job to do the wash, clean the house, and be primarily responsible for taking care of the children and you. You generally know where she has been and what she's been doing. You can see if her arms are full or free. You know what time of the day it is and what needs to be done around the house. You can certainly tell if she's tired. From these and many other things that you know about your best friend, you can draw certain assumptions about what she's thinking and what she needs.

If you're not paying attention, you can't anticipate her needs. That's exactly my point. You must remain aware of what's going on in your partner's life by looking at her with an eye toward helping her if you see a chance to do something that could make the moment slightly easier for her. If you really want to be her best friend, anticipating her needs should be no big deal. For her, though, it's a *huge* deal. If you are anticipating her needs, she'll anticipate every single one of yours. You simply won't believe how good life can be.

■ ASK HER IF HER DAY WAS A GOOD ONE AND LISTEN ATTENTIVELY EVEN IF YOU KNOW WHAT SHE'S GOING TO SAY

It's not a matter of being insecure, but she wants to be reassured, as often as possible, that you are her best friend. You can do this by listening attentively to her. You must do this with perfect eye contact without glancing at the television even for a moment. You must do this without being interrupted by anyone or anything until she's finished and you must sincerely be interested and listen attentively.

Yes, she may be slow in telling you something that in one form or another you've heard a hundred times. Don't kid yourself. She knows she's taking her good ol' time to tell you what she wants to say. She knows you've heard it before. She probably even knows that your mind is wandering even though you look like it isn't. But she thinks to herself, "He's such a good listener," and she thinks that you're precious for trying to act as though you're interested.

■ NEVER YELL AT HER

Why in the world would you ever intentionally inflict pain on your best friend? We can't think of any good or even lousy reason. So don't yell at her. There is no excuse. "I'm sorry" won't work. If you've yelled at her, you might as well have hit her with a right cross. To her, you did. "It was no big deal," you say. Wanna bet?

APPENDIX
B

A Woman's Guide to Being a Man's Best Friend

INTRODUCTION

$\mathcal{A}$lthough I didn't provide an introduction to Appendix A, *A Man's Guide To Being A Woman's Best Friend,* I feel it's important to share a few thoughts before I become specific with regard to this quick reference guide. Remember earlier that I mentioned that "Women inherently seem to know how to be a man's best friend." With few exceptions, women don't need a guide. That doesn't mean to say that they are all perfect. There are those who have character flaws and hopefully are working to overcome them. In general, though, if a man does everything in *A Man's Guide To Being A Woman's Best Friend* every day of his life, women will respond by giving back tenfold. Women love to give to their man.

On the other hand, if her man doesn't tell the truth about everything; if he doesn't appreciate that if she's working outside the home she is really carrying four and maybe five full-time jobs, especially if she has children; and if he evidences abandonment-causing behaviors frequently — look out! Most women are much more vicious than most men. So, in spite of the fact that women inherently seem to know how to be a man's best friend, this appendix is intended to *provide insights* for women with that inherent knowledge — enabling them to "give" to their man even better than before.

As a result, because you've chosen to be with a man who "gets it," you'll have more fun and will be treated even better by him.

Okay. I know this next statement leads to a sensitive subject, but since I've openly shared my perspective with you throughout this book, I won't feel good about not including this last — but to me, my most important — perspective. I believe that most women are stronger, more clear-thinking, and smarter than most men. To be really truthful, I believe women are *all* smarter than most men, especially if they are loved in the way they should be loved and made to feel special. I believe that a man cannot effectively "get through life" without a woman who helps him to think more clearly. I believe that men — including me (although I've been trained a little better than most) think too much of the time with certain parts of their body other than with their brain, if you get my drift.

So as you begin to read this final section of *Best Friends Forever,* keep this in mind. If he's not being your best friend, don't bother trying to be his (and, of course, if a woman is not being a man's best friend, that's true for men, too). Life is too short to give, give, and then give some more to any man who doesn't choose to respond appropriately.

It's better to be your own best friend and give to yourself while being alone, than to waste your life giving much of yourself to a guy who thinks that simply "having a woman" makes him big, strong, powerful, and smarter.

■ BE GOOD TO YOURSELF SO YOU CAN FEEL GOOD ABOUT BEING GOOD TO HIM

For you to be your best, and for you to grow to become the person you were destined to become, you must be selfish more than just once in a while. I know that men get up in the morning too, in order to fight the dragons that we all must fight to make a living. But do they have to whine about how tired they are at the end of the day, everyday? Do they have to expect to be waited on, hand and foot, just because they, too, worked hard for eight to ten hours? Here's another reality check. In the majority of cases, women also work outside the home. And whether or not they work outside the home, they *still* feel they are primarily responsible for taking care of the children, the house, doing the wash, preparing dinners, and coordinating most aspects of the family's entire life. How many jobs is that? It's a whole lot more than "one." So get a manicure and pedicure often. Buy that special moisturizer you want. Take time to work out or go to a yoga class a few times a week. Take time to read a book every day. Life will go on. Things will get done. He's capable of helping to fill in for you when you're taking time for yourself. And if he doesn't help out when you need him to help — *without you asking* — don't wash his underwear. Maybe next time he'll drive the kids to baseball practice or help them with their homework. Maybe next time he'll wash the dirty dishes that are in the sink or he'll empty the dishwasher when it's full of clean dishes. And if he's smart, maybe next time he'll take you out to dinner when you haven't had time to prepare any because you took the time to be good to yourself.

I present myself to you
in a form suitable to the relationship
I wish to achieve with you.
— Luigi Pirandello, 1867–1936

■ ALWAYS TELL THE TRUTH, EVEN ABOUT THE SMALLEST DETAIL

Earlier I said that women inherently know when their man is not truthful. Well, generally it takes men a light year or two to know when their woman is not telling the truth. When they finally figure it out, though, they will feel betrayed. He'll begin to distrust you when it comes to everything.

He'll stop following *The Man's Guide To Being A Woman's Best Friend* and you will have reason to feel abandoned. If you can't tell him the truth about everything, don't be with him.

The future is purchased by the present.
— Dr. Samuel Johnson, 1709–1784

■ TRUST THAT HE WILL ALWAYS TELL YOU THE TRUTH

Certainly it takes years of consistent behavior for any of us to trust another person. But, if he's openly sharing everything he does during the day and is being honest and objective about himself and the quality of his daily accomplishments, trust that he will always tell you the truth. You'll instinctively know when something he says seems amiss and of course you'll ask a follow up question or two. But in general remember that trust begets honesty. Whereas if you seem to be questioning everything he says and you make him feel as though you don't trust him, he may end up giving you reason to distrust him.

■ UNDERSTAND THE PRESSURE HE FEELS TO BE THE PRIMARY WAGE EARNER

From his perspective, he's got to be your hero. Again, he feels that he's the one who must earn enough money to buy a beautiful home. He's the one responsible for going into the wilderness to hunt for food. Our society has taught him to believe that he's supposed to be the primary wage earner. We know that is not true in today's world, but he'll always believe it's true — and that's not a bad thing for him to be feeling.

If you earn more money than he earns, to him, his penis may feel inadequate. (Don't laugh, it's true!) Realistically, even if you fight the feeling, you may feel slightly disappointed, too. Don't ever let that feeling show, even when you're angry. If you do, he'll not only feel that his penis is small, he'll feel like it's been cut off. That's not a good thing for either you *or* him.

> *When we feel that we lack whatever is needed to secure someone else's esteem, we are very close to hating him.*
> — Luc de Clapiers de Vauvenargues, 1715–1747

■ LET HIM KNOW THAT HIS BEST IS GOOD ENOUGH

If you use phrases like "my car is good enough," "I don't need that outfit now," or "I don't need that purse anyway," he'll wish he could do more for you and he may be disappointed in himself. There are no words to help him to feel better about himself. It's all about how you look at him. It's about how you touch his face as you smile softly and lovingly when you're letting him know that you love him.

Your words, although well meaning, could backfire. Say "thank you" to him once in a while when the words "thank you" aren't normally the words you'd use in the context of what's going on. For example, you might say "thank you" as you kiss him goodbye in the morning. You might walk over to him when he's had to bring some work home to catch up and gently touch him while saying "thank you."

He'll feel what you're telling him; that you know he's doing his best and it's fine, whatever it is. Be his friend, especially if he is being your best friend, too.

Many men are like unto sausages:
Whatever you stuff them with,
that they will bear in them.
— Alexi Konstantinovich Tolstoy 1817–1875

■ LET HIM KNOW THAT IT'S OKAY NOT TO ALWAYS BE STRONG

He needs to feel safe in your presence. You've got to allow him to feel comfortable whimpering just a little as he crawls into bed with you at night and cuddles up behind you in the morning. You've got to allow him to tell you that he's afraid, that he's tired, that he's disappointed he's not accomplishing more. Remember that he wants to be your knight in shining armor. He expects it of himself. Hold him as you'd hold your baby. He *is* your baby, you know. Men never lose the need to be mothered, no matter how old they are. Never forget: in some ways he'll always be a little boy needing to be held by his mom. Do that for him. He'll try even harder to be your hero.

■ DON'T TRY TO CHANGE HIM

It doesn't work.

> *Be not angry that you cannot make others*
> *as you wish them to be,*
> *since you cannot make yourself*
> *as you wish to be.*
> — Thomas a Kempis 1380–1471

■ UNDERSTAND THAT IN SOME WAYS HE'LL ALWAYS BE A LITTLE BOY

Take advantage of it.

■ DON'T EVER BE DEMANDING

Except when it's important for both of you.

> *Never claim as a right*
> *what you can ask as a favor.*
> — John Churton Collins, 1848–1908

■ **BE HIS FANTASY**

You were his fantasy when you first met him. The look in your eyes said "Play with me, I'll be anything you want." Throughout your relationship, he'll always remember how you dropped your keys — accidentally of course — while walking in front of him and then you had to bend down in that special way to pick them up. He'll remember how you stripped for him. He'll remember the sounds you made when he kissed you passionately.

You were his fantasy in the beginning. Be his fantasy as often as you can muster up the energy to be his fantasy. It doesn't have to be that often. It has to be just often enough to remind him that "you can make him tingle" just by the way you look at him — and certainly by the way you play with him.

One does what one is; one becomes what one does.
— Robert von Musil 1880–1942

■ **UNDERSTAND HIS NEED TO SHOW OFF A LITTLE**

He'll never outgrow it. Get used to it. Hopefully, you'll love him enough to think it's cute. Play it up big, baby. Tell him how strong he is and how impressed you are with his athleticism. I hate to admit it, but every one of us is so stupid when it comes to that stuff. Play into that stupidity. He'll love that you do that for him. I know it seems impossible, but it'll make him less "stupid" about the important things in life.

■ LET HIM MAKE THE CHOICE WHEN THE CHOICE ISN'T REALLY IMPORTANT TO YOU

Does it really matter where you go for dinner, or what movie you see? Does it really matter if he asks you to wear a particular fragrance, though you'd choose a different one? Does it matter if the car you're buying is white or burgundy; Ford or Chevrolet; Mercedes, Jaguar, or BMW?

If he's generally doing everything described in *A Man's Guide to Being A Woman's Best Friend* (Appendix A), then allow him to make the decisions when those decisions are not the really, really important ones. Be easy for him. In turn, he'll be low maintenance for you.

■ BABY HIM WHEN HE DOESN'T FEEL WELL

I don't know any other way to put this than "men feel the weight of the world" on their shoulders much more than women. Perhaps it goes back to my belief that women are stronger, more clear-thinking, etc. Certainly we know that attempting to complete each and every one of *your* responsibilities while having cramps each month isn't easy. We know that being pregnant for nine months while still being responsible for every aspect of "the world of your life" isn't fair. There probably isn't a man living who could climb that mountain. And it's very true that having a runny nose shouldn't incapacitate a big, strong, intelligent man like your partner. But a little cough, chest cold, and runny nose causes most men to feel — no, make that *act* — like their life is coming to an end.

I can't provide a logical explanation for babying him when he doesn't feel well.

I just know that he needs you to do it. So, you know what? Accept this one on face value. I haven't suggested that you do this before, so if he really is trying his best and his best generally is good enough, tolerate his low tolerance for discomfort and baby him. Don't baby him too seriously, though. Bring him some juice, a decongestant, a box of tissues, and plug in a video of his favorite cowboy movie. That's enough. You've got the really important stuff to do.

■ SEND HIM LOVING CARDS OR MESSAGES AT WORK

If you do this, he'll smile a little as he reads them. He'll set them on his desk amongst the pictures he has of you and the children. Once in a while he'll glance at them and remember how much he's loved. And anyone who walks by his desk and even glances at what's there — for even just a moment — will know that *this* man is someone else's territory, and the woman to whom he belongs will protect her territory with a vengeance if necessary.

Send the message to him as well as to anyone else who has the unmitigated nerve to look at his personal stuff.

> *Anybody who believes that the way to a man's heart*
> *is through his stomach flunked geography.*
> — Robert Byrne 1930–

■ YOU DON'T ALWAYS HAVE TO BE RIGHT

If you have to prove you're right and he's wrong, in the long run you're the wrong one for him. Who cares who's right? The two of you are partners. As long as one of you is right, it doesn't have to be you. Be easy for him — especially if he's being easy for you.

> *You lose it if you talk about it.*
> — Ernest Hemingway 1899–1961

■ ENCOURAGE HIM TO FANTASIZE

He'll be more playful with you. And, oh yes — you may not have to be available to him sexually so much of the time if you don't feel like it. Tell him stories in the kind of voice you'd be talking to him with if he were on the other end of the 900 number some of his friends call. You know the kind of voice I'm describing. "When you were 15 years old and you had this little neighbor girl who thought you were so cute and she loved to wear old, a little bit too small, cutoffs with a little tee-shirt that was short and showed her midriff. And one day, when she saw your mom leave the house — perhaps to go shopping — and she knew you were alone, she came over to your house to see if you had seen her history book that she thought she left at your house the last time she was there." That's the kind of story I mean. Do you want me to describe the story further? Ask my wife to do it. She's the one with the imagination.

■ COMPROMISE EASILY

It's probably not too difficult to imagine the world these days, outside of your home, as a big, bad place. It's really a scary place to be for most of us. Oh sure, we all pretend we're secure, confident, happy, centered, and so on and so forth. But the truth is we all struggle.

We struggle financially, regardless of how many zeros there are at the end of our annual income. We struggle emotionally. Most of us have some baggage we carry with us from traumatic things that were said or done to us during our lives. We struggle to become better human beings every day. We struggle to maintain healthy relationships, both at work and with our friends. Just trying to keep up with all the things we have to do each day is a struggle.

So when it comes to you and your best friend, your partner, the one with whom you've chosen to spend the rest of your life, be easy. That, of course, goes for him, too. Compromise easily when it comes to the minor things. Try to peacefully find common ground when it relates to the big things. You two are working together to survive in this big, bad world of ours, so you both need to compromise easily. You can only really survive with peace and happiness if it's easy to be peaceful with your partner. Pick your spots to make a stand. But try not to make that stand on too many issues. Move easily toward that center point. Teach him to do it, too. It'll help to make being "Best Friends Forever" really attainable instead of just a fantasy.

■ PUT YOUR ARM INSIDE HIS AS YOU WALK BESIDE HIM

Be "his" girl. He wants you to be "his" girl. He loves the feeling. Allow yourself to let him feel what he needs to feel.

■ **ARRANGE HIS PILLOWS AS HE
GETS READY TO FALL ASLEEP**

You know it's just a few seconds away from the time the two of you put your heads down for the night. You reach over and arrange his pillow(s) in the position you know he feels most comfortable. You reach over and place your hand on his head and gently move him down toward the pillows. You pull the covers up above his shoulders and tuck him in. He's now cuddled down for the night. He whispers "I love you, honey," and he's off to sleep.

■ **GIVE HIM A MASSAGE**

It's as good as sex.

■ **LET HIM KNOW THAT STAYING HOME
ON A SATURDAY NIGHT CAN BE PERFECT**

He's tired. He might have even worked that day, too. He knows that Saturday night is generally the night the two of you go out to play. Once in a while, maybe even *more* than once in a while, light some candles. Give him a glass of wine. Turn the lights down low. Kiss his forehead and say, "We're staying home tonight." Hopefully by now, if you've read this book together, he's learned that you know best anyway. So he sighs, says "thank you" and later that night he massages your feet (or better!).

■ **DON'T SHOP FOR CLOTHES WHEN YOU KNOW HE'S
UNDER FINANCIAL PRESSURE**

Is that too obvious to be in this book at this point? Maybe so, but I feel it needs to be said.

■ **INCLUDE HIS FAVORITE FOODS IN YOUR SHOPPING LIST**

He won't tell you that he noticed you were thinking of him as you walked through the market, but he'll know that you wanted to please him.

■ BE SURE HE KNOWS THAT YOU ARE PROUD OF HIM

Okay, so not everything he does is perfect. There is no such thing as a perfect man. He may really be trying to be everything he promised you he'd try to be, though.

If he is really trying — and most of the time succeeding — actually *tell* him that you're proud to be his wife, partner, or best friend.

■ NEVER EMBARRASS HIM

Anything you say in front of others — or just to him — that embarrasses him is a major breach of trust. It's a major breach of friendship. To him it plays directly into his insecurity. It's important to remember that even though we may pretend we're wonderfully intelligent, aggressive, athletic, and so forth, down deep we don't really believe it. It has nothing to do with the reality of our performance. We all think that we're less good looking, less smart, less capable of making lots of money, and deficient when it comes to making love to you and comparing ourselves to whoever in the world we perceive are the "big time winners." Does all this relate to a man's perception of the size of his penis? Of course it does!

If you say anything to him that touches one of those "insecurity spots," it undermines the confidence he has in himself that he works so hard, every day, to maintain. Of course, down deep, when he's really being honest with himself, he knows the truth. But he feels angry that you, the person he trusts the most not to uncover his vulnerability, said something that "blew his cover."

The problem is not that momentarily he will feel vulnerable — the real problem will be his reaction to what you said. Your words will elicit an angry response from him, and that response will be aimed at one of your vulnerable spots. An argument ensues, and most often a couple won't be able to see through the reality of what took place. You each add another brick to your respective barriers and life goes on, with the two of you a little less "in touch."

I have to say, though, if you have a really good base established of trust — and you really are Best Friends — a little poke now and then won't cause any damage and should elicit the funny moment it was meant to generate.

Here's a personal example of what I'm referring to. Susan and I were getting ready to go to brunch one Sunday morning at our friends Noreen and Howard's home. Now you have to understand that, at 51 years of age, in 30 minutes — no matter at what point she's at — Susan shines. She is truly the most beautiful, brightest human being I've ever met. Anyway, she is a woman — and because she's a woman and as such so very bright, she can be dangerously and devastatingly quick. So basically, I just don't mess with her, even playfully. This one morning I could see out of the corner of my eye that it was going to take her just a little longer to "shine." I'm in the bathroom looking in my mirror, she's on the other side of the bathroom looking in her mirror, and I think to myself, "Do I dare say anything?" I then think, "What the hell, let's play." So I say "Honey," (just the way I said "honey" she knew something was coming) "Do you think that you can get it together in about 30 minutes?" She whips around and within one fraction of a second says to me "Do you think you can lose 30 pounds in 30 minutes?"

Now come on. How funny and brilliant and absolutely magnificent is that? We both laughed hard. I trust Susan and she trusts me. (Although she doesn't trust that I won't open my big mouth and tell the world stories like I just did.) But you've got to be patient to get your man to the point where his vulnerable spots can be tickled — not poked — by an "exposing" remark. Understand how fragile men really are, regardless of how we pretend to be otherwise. Be his best friend. Stroke him a little. I'm sure you understand what I mean. Incidentally, I recently lost 30 pounds...good stroking, huh?

■ DON'T COMPARE HIM TO OTHER MEN

To him, comparing him to other men comes in many forms. You might innocently say "He has nice hair," "He smells so good," "He's so polite," "He dresses so nicely," or "That's a really nice car he's driving." You might say "I wish we lived in such a nice house" or "He must have a really good job." He hears your words differently than you mean them. He hears "His hair is nicer than your hair," "I wish you smelled good like him," "You don't say or do those things for me," or "You don't look that great in your clothes," etc. Your words may trigger his feelings of inadequacy. Remember, as I mentioned earlier, it doesn't matter how secure he looks or acts, he's still not sure that he's "all that."

■ LISTEN TO HIM WITHOUT INTERRUPTING

Generally, he'll want to talk about his job or something that's happened at work. Unlike with you, listening to him is not foreplay. It's his reward for going out each day to slay the dragons. He needs to be rewarded. Listening to him, sympathizing with him, making him feel like you understand how difficult it all is, makes him feel that you appreciate what he's doing for you and your family each day. Sure, I know that it sounds like I'm saying he's like a little boy who needs your approval. Well, yes — I am saying just that. I know that I'm saying just what you think most of the time anyway. So don't be so disappointed that your big, strong knight in shining armor is really a little boy dressed up in shining armor needing to be told how cute and yet powerful he looks. Accept it. It's a fact. Nearly all of us are little boys pretending to be all grown up. We'll try harder for you if you understand that we need to be held, comforted, and told we're really doing a good job. It's not about listening, as it is with you. It's about comforting him and letting him know that you appreciate the struggles he faces each day.

■ BE PATIENT WHEN HE WANTS TO WATCH HIS FAVORITE SPORTS ON TV

Only if he's being your best friend.

■ MAKE GOOD EYE CONTACT WITH HIM AND HELP HIM TO DO THE SAME

Perfect eye contact is critical. You can see into his soul if his eye contact is good. If he continually looks away from you, *gently* touch his face and move his head back to the position where you can see his eyes. Tell him that you can undertstand what he's saying better if you can see his eyes. Teach him. He needs to be taught. We all need to be taught. Be his friend. Teach him to be his best. If he's not teachable, dump him.

■ LIGHT CANDLES IN YOUR BEDROOM BEFORE GOING TO BED

You don't think this is important? Try it and see how much sexier your room feels when you get into bed at night.

■ TELL HIM THAT HE'S THE BEST YOU'VE EVER HAD

Lie if you have to. He just needs to hear the words. If you do, though, he'll always *want* to be the best you've ever had.

■ ESTABLISH AND LIVE WITHIN YOUR BUDGET

Neither you nor he can be at peace with yourselves or one another if together you spend more money than your income permits. Everything in your life together may be wonderful. You may be achieving the highest level of success at being his best friend. You will not, however, be able to eliminate as many levels of his anxiety as you would like to eliminate unless you successfully live within a responsibly established budget that the two of you establish together.

If you are unable to meet your financial responsibilities, seek help *together* from a consumer credit counseling organization or a financial advisor, and *together* make those difficult decisions that most of us, at some time in our life, must make. Include him in all of those decisions so that he understands that unless your financial state of affairs is well balanced, the two of you will not be able to connect as freely and comfortably as you would like.

■ RUN A BUBBLE BATH FOR HIM

If you want to make him feel loved just a little bit extra, run a bath for him, put bubbles in it, light candles and place them around the tub, and put a towel in the dryer so that it's hot when it's time for him to dry off.

■ BE HIS PLAYMATE

From time to time, glance deeply and carefully into his eyes. Touch his face gently with your hand. He loves it when you do that. If you are being his friend in the sense we are describing, you will almost always be able to create within him the twinkle that he's waiting for you to bring out in him. Allow your twinkle to play with his twinkle and you'll find that the two of you will be making love without being in bed, and smiling at each other much more.

■ TAKE A SHOWER WITH HIM

Of course, this isn't something you do with him or for him daily. It's a once in a while thing you do because it can be a playful thing for both of you. Allow him to help you dry yourself off and you do the same for him. It's fun. It may have been something you did while you were first dating. It will remind him of the excitement he felt while you were first dating. It can help to sustain the sensuous part of your relationship.

■ MAKE SURE HE EATS BREAKFAST AND TAKES HIS VITAMIN PILLS

He's rushing to get ready to go to work. Perhaps he's exercised, caught up on some work he'd brought home with him, taken a shower, and dressed. You both know that he's got to be at work shortly. Hand him his vitamin pills, a glass of water, and a banana if that's all you have time to do. If there's a little more time, put a bowl of cereal in front of him with a glass of orange juice and say "Sit down and eat." He'll get the message: you want him to have enough energy to feel good during his day. You love him and want him to be healthy. If you do this consistently, he'll honestly hear those words without you having to verbalize them.

■ SUGGEST CHANGES RATHER THAN COMPLAINING

I don't know how often I've heard both men and women say during mediation, "Nothing I do is good enough." Of course, by the time a couple gets to mediation, barriers have been built. Very little each of them does for the other seems acceptable. Each is feeling too much anger at themselves for the things they did that brought them to the point of dissolving their marriage and anger at their partner for the things that they did. Each is feeling remorseful and they're both experiencing the difficult time we have "making ends meet financially" and being able to succeed at the balancing act we all go through every day of our lives trying to get done everything we need to get done. By the time a couple gets to my office each has good reason to complain.

It's easy, especially when we're tired, to find things that we wish were a little different.

So suggest changes rather than complaining. Suppose he's dirty when he walks in the door after work and doesn't wash his hands, but instead sits down at the dinner table. You might say to him "How can you sit down for dinner when you're so dirty?" or you could say "Honey, you might feel a little more refreshed if you cleaned up a little." Perhaps you're going out on a Saturday night and he wants to go to the movies. You want to go dancing. It may not be a good idea to say, "We always have to do what *you* want to do." Try this instead: "Honey, it might be fun if we go dancing tonight."

I know it shouldn't be so much work even having to think about your choice of words, but for many a man, critical words may remind him of the way that his mother spoke to him. If your man was raised by a mother who seemed not easy to please, any button you push that makes him feel like you are disapproving of his behavior will cause him to react angrily. So think about your choice of words. This suggestion is, of course, equally true for men.

■ TELL HIM TO BE SAFE AS YOU KISS HIM GOODBYE IN THE MORNING

This is another way of saying, "I love you." It tells him that you cherish sharing your life with him, and that you understand how dangerous our world has become. It tells him that you want him to pay attention to everything going on around him, so that you're safely back together again that evening.

■ TELL HIM HE'S *SOOOO* BIG AND STRONG

Men (and I'm embarrassed to say I'm definitely included) are so gullible when it comes to hearing a woman say "Oh, wow, you're amazing, you're so big, oh my, ohhhhhh!" So big deal: Tell him what he needs to hear — most of us go to sleep afterwards anyway, while you laugh quietly to yourself about the fact that he really believes you.

■ CARESS HIM OFTEN

Men need to be caressed often, just as you do. Caressing him often makes him feel that he is still attractive to you. It feels good, too.

■ LET HIM PAT POWDER ON YOU AFTER YOU SHOWER

As young boys, most men looked at *Playboy* and pictures of nude women. It excited them. As men, if we've invaded your privacy anyway and you're at a point where you're about ready to powder yourself, ask him to pat powder on you. He'll love that you do that for him. It's just another something you can do to be his playmate.

■ THANK HIM FOR WORKING SO HARD

It's important to remember that most men honestly believe that their work is more difficult than your work. It's so untrue that it's unimaginable to me that any man could possibly *believe* that it's true, but men really believe it. It's not that men are stupid, it's that men have not been designed to carry four or five full-time jobs. Working outside the home is one job. Feeling primarily responsible for meals, doing the wash, cleaning the house, following up when the credit card, utility and telephone bills are incorrect, and driving the children from place to place is job number two. Being primarily responsible for raising the children is number three. Raising *him* is number four, and somehow making time for themselves is number five. As little boys, most men watch their mothers do all of those jobs. As little girls, most women watched as their mothers worked themselves to the point of exhaustion and girls just expected that one day they would do all of those things, too. Men expected that their partner would be responsible for five full-time jobs. Women, over their lifetime, conditioned themselves to being able to handle all of those responsibilities and somehow get through it daily. Men, throughout their lifetime, were conditioned to believe that they are primarily responsible for making a good living and are exhausted by even *thinking* about the prospect of doing more. (Notwithstanding the foregoing, men really *do* feel a lot of pressure as they compete everyday to make more money.)

The words "thank you" are nice for you to hear from him and for him to hear from you. They're especially nice to say when there doesn't seem to be any reason to be saying them. This "thank you" is a different "thank you" than the one said when he brings you a glass of water or clears the dishes from the table after dinner. He'll know what you mean. Try it.

■ KISS HIM OFTEN ON HIS LIPS

Kissing him on his lips — and I mean *really* kissing him, is a sensuous thing to do for him. It makes him tingle. It's something he feels throughout his entire day. It's a great way to say "goodbye" in the morning or "hello, you big handsome stud" in the evening when you see him again. Kisses on the cheek are for "mothers-in-law," not him. No, I don't mean you have to "put out" every time that you kiss him, but I'm suggesting that you don't forget to intersperse your kisses with the special, "I love you baby and I want you to love me, baby" kisses.

■ DON'T YELL AT HIM

Try to remember that, in his mind, "he's the man" — even though he questions the reality of it (only to himself) daily. If you yell at him, he'll become defensive. His mother probably yelled at him. When she yelled at him he reluctantly did what she wanted him to do. When you yell at him it reminds him of the times when his mother yelled at him and he wanted to yell back but suppressed the urge to do so. He *will* yell back at you. So be careful, please — try to remember that even though you're exhausted almost every moment of every day that "asking gently" works better. If asking gently doesn't work, open this book to Appendix A and say, "Honey, do me a favor. Would you read all of this for me?" If that doesn't work, and you still have to yell at him to help you, then stop yelling anyway. Accept the really positive parts of him and give up the effort to change him. If you can't do that, be his best friend and your own best friend, too — and, as sad as this sounds, think about making a major change in your life.

■ WEAR A FRAGRANCE HE LIKES

There are fragrances you love and fragrances you wear that elicit a positive "You smell good." Wear his favorites more of the time when you're with him. Wear *your* favorites when you're at work, shopping, or going out with your girlfriend.

■ LET HIM CHOOSE THE CAR HE WANTS TO BUY

Provided the cost of it is not more excessive than is affordable for the two of you.

■ DON'T EVER IMPLY YOU WISH HE EARNED MORE MONEY

His ego is more fragile than you ever imagined. We all know that none of us can ever make "enough" money. We all struggle to pay all our bills and still be able to afford all those nice things we'd like to own. He is really sensitive to the slightest indication that you wish he could earn more money. He feels that you don't appreciate how hard he is trying. He feels your lack of consideration for how hard he's trying to improve his earning capacity. Now, if he's copping out of trying doing his best every day, that's a different story. But remember: don't complain — suggest changes. Help him think through the problem. Your perspective is clearer than his is. Share it with him really *gently*. He's feeling the same frustration you feel about not having enough money to "keep up" with your ever-growing expenses. Out-think his defensiveness. Choose your words carefully.

■ DON'T CHECK UP ON HIM

Well, let's see. If you're checking up on him it's probably because you're feeling really insecure about yourself and projecting that feeling of insecurity onto him — or you believe he's not telling you the truth. If you're feeling insecure about yourself, get to work on the biggest struggle we all experience in life — that struggle to become the person we always wanted to become. I realize that's easier said than done. But be careful that you're not projecting your feelings of insecurity onto him before you start playing detective.

On the other hand, if you're checking up on him because you sense he's not telling you the truth, remember that you may actually find out the truth. Is that a bad thing? No.

But if he's not telling you the truth, then he's not being your best friend, and you've already begun building barriers that shelter you from him. He's probably not feeling loved either because of those barriers you built, and he's begun to build his own barriers because of that. So what's checking up on him got to do with it? When you begin to check up on him you venture into what could very well be a final stage of your relationship with him. Be sure you're ready to go there before you choose this direction.

■ PREPARE THE COFFEE MAKER SO IT'S READY FOR HIM IN THE MORNING

If he gets up earlier than you do in the morning and he likes to have his coffee when he awakens, it's nice for him to simply be able to click on the coffee maker and know that in minutes it'll be ready. It takes a little extra effort when you're exhausted and ready for bed yourself but he will appreciate it.

■ EXERCISE REGULARLY AND ENCOURAGE
HIM TO DO SO ALSO

You don't have to become frumpy, you know. He doesn't have to become flabby either. Set some time aside to exercise together if you're able to do so. If not, take that selfish time I spoke of earlier. Encourage him to take that time, too. In addition to keeping him healthy, it'll give you the space you need from him so you can take a deep breath — and maybe a bubble bath, too.

■ ENCOURAGE HIM TO STAY IN TOUCH WITH HIS FAMILY

Some men will naturally want to stay in touch with members of their family, and they will do so. Other men want to stay in touch, but forget to do so. Still others can't stand to even speak on the telephone to certain members of their family. If your man wants to stay in touch with members of his family, he doesn't need encouragement to do so. For those of you who are with men who *know* they should keep in touch, but put it off, a gentle reminder now and then is a good idea. And if you are married to one of those men, if he's too busy or puts it off for whatever reason, once in a while make the calls for him — if only to just say "Hi, we were thinking about you." He'll really appreciate that you do that for him. Don't cover for him too often, though. He should be making those calls himself.

If you are partners with a man who can't stand to even *think* about his family, let alone speak with them, you may be experiencing problems with him that go far deeper than "just encouraging him to stay in touch with his family." In these instances, encourage him to seek the help of a therapist who is able to help him get over the anger he feels at both members of his family and perhaps even at himself.

If he's really angry with others and perhaps with himself, that anger inhibits his ability to freely love you the way you should be and need to be loved.

■ **ENCOURAGE HIM TO GO OUT WITH HIS FRIENDS**

As long as he and his friends play nicely together.

■ **ACCEPT HIS NEED FOR SEXUAL RELEASE IF...**

Now this topic — for me at least — may be difficult to explain. It's somewhat obvious that most men have masturbated since they've been teenagers; and masturbation is "fine" but it's not exactly like the other stuff that's really fun. I'm not completely certain that women also don't have a frequent need for sexual release. So what I'm trying to say rather clumsily is, please don't hold it against me if I'm discussing this topic as though it's exclusively a "man thing."

Please try not to feel disgusted by his need to masturbate. Try not to feel as though you're less than adequate for him in a sexual context. In other words, don't take the fact that he masturbates personally. For most men, it has nothing to do with the quality of your sexual relationship or the number of times each month you have sex. For most men masturbation is much more of an emotional release rather than a sexual release.

It's a very brief vacation from the pressure he feels to earn a good living and fulfill all of his other obligations. It's not a reflection of any deficiency in you. If you allow yourself to feel that his need to masturbate relates to your lack of being able to please him, it may inhibit your ability to be peaceful about having sex with him. That will detract from your own enjoyment and may cause him to feel inadequate about his being able to please you while the two of you are making love.

■ LET HIM KNOW HE MAKES YOU FEEL GOOD

Perhaps you do this by sending little notes or cards to him at work. Perhaps you do it by saying the words "thank you" when it's not necessarily appropriate to say "thank you." Maybe it's that you remember to tell him to take his vitamins or tell him to be safe as he leaves for work. There are many ways to let him know that he makes you feel good. Of course, the best one is to permit him to sleep in your bed each night.

■ ENCOURAGE HIM TO REACH FOR HIS DREAMS

I dream of the day when the divorce rate is 25% rather than 50%. I dream of the day when we all donate four hours of our time, every year, doing anything we can do for charity (*see www.servicexchange.org*). I dream of the day when we all record the story of our lifetime so our great-grandchildren will be able to learn everything about us, not just be able to see pictures of us (see *www.playinheritance.com* — coming fall of 2002) If he's a dreamer, encourage him to reach for his dreams — provided it doesn't force the two of you into bankruptcy. Encouraging him to reach for his dreams is one of the best rewards you can give him for being your best friend.

■ NEVER SAY ANYTHING THAT WOULD MAKE HIM FEEL UNWORTHY

We are all sensitive to negative input, especially from someone we love. Anytime you say things like "You're lazy," "You're sloppy," "You're a pig," or "Why can't you earn more money?", he will shut down emotionally in order to protect himself from being hurt by you again. Verbal abuse is as devastating as physical abuse. If you say things that cause him to feel unworthy, he might go through the motions of being with you — perhaps even for years — but you've hurt him, you've not been his friend, and he will retaliate by saying things to you that are intended to make you feel unworthy.

■ MAKE SURE HE HAS REGULAR PHYSICAL CHECK-UPS

Most women take it for granted they will go to their gyne-cologist at least once a year. They'll have a mammogram. To a woman, the discomfort of being examined by their doctor is simply something they must do for themselves regularly. Most men are just the opposite. They have to be so sick they're sure they are dying before they'll go to a doctor. Don't just remind him to make that appointment to see his doctor; tell him he can't come home that night unless he does so.

■ UNDERSTAND AND BE PATIENT WITH HIS INSECURITY IF YOU EARN MORE MONEY THAN HE EARNS

I'm not saying that you have to like it. I'm only saying that although he suppresses the feeling, it probably makes him slightly nauseous — especially if he wants to always be your knight in shining armor. So the question is, "What are you to do if you really do earn more or even much more money than he earns?" Make it seem irrelevant. The two of you are a team. You're bound together for eternity. Which one of you earns more money, which one puts the children to sleep, which one writes the checks to pay the bills, or which one does the grocery shop-ping is completely irrelevant. If you earn more money than he earns, make certain that he understands this concept.

If he equates making more money with being smarter, and if you earn more money than he earns, then he's far ahead of most men and you're lucky. He understands the primary point behind my perception expressed in *Best Friends Forever*. Most women are far smarter, more clear-thinking, and stronger in every way than most men. Nevertheless, be gentle and understand that he wishes you didn't have to work if you chose not to. He really wants to be your hero.

■ BE PATIENT WHILE HE'S LEARNING
TO BE YOUR BEST FRIEND

Provided he's teachable, be patient. For example, if you say to him, "Would you please wipe the water marks off of the mirror and wipe the bathroom sink when you finish shaving in the morning?" and after you ask him he does it consistently, he's teachable. If you say, "Please don't share our entire lives with our friends next time we go out with them" and from then on he shares only *half* of your entire lives, he's teachable. For some of us it takes more time than it should. But if you're patient and he loves you enough to be teachable, someday he'll be a "keeper."

■ IF HE'S NOT TRYING TO BE YOUR BEST FRIEND FORGIVE
YOURSELF FOR NOT WANTING TO BE HIS

Hopefully, you're not at the point in your relationship where each of you has built barriers that prevent you and your partner from connecting with one another and being best friends. If you *are* at this point in your relationship, though, you may be feeling that you yelled back at him too much of the time or you were too critical, and that at least *some* element of the problems that exist have been caused by you. Indeed, the truth *may be* that at least some of the problems have been caused by you. But now it's time for you to be introspective and objective. It's time to read the headings of Appendix A located just prior to this appendix and ask yourself this question: "If he did everything contained in *A Man's Guide to Being A Woman's Best Friend* every day, would I have been his best friend, too — in the truest sense of the words?"

So turn to Appendix A and close your eyes for just a minute or two. Allow yourself to go back in time to the moment when you first met, and picture him doing everything (and I mean *everything*) contained in *A Man's Guide* every day of your lives together. After you've completed reading only the headings of that section, ask yourself this question: "If he did everything contained in that section every day, would I have been critical of him? Would I have yelled at him? Or would I have given him the best of myself everyday of our relationship?"

If he didn't do 99% of everything contained in *A Man's Guide To Being A Woman's Best Friend*, you probably had good reasons for being angry with him. You would not have yelled or been critical of him. So, since he hasn't consistently been your best friend, forgive yourself for not wanting to be his.

APPENDIX C

Best Friends Forever Wedding Vow

With this ring my sweet love, I thee wed.

In doing so I promise to be your best friend forever.

I promise to carefully listen to
and accept your perspective
and always compromise mine.

I promise to maintain a heightened awareness
so I can anticipate your needs.

I promise to hold you close and never cause you
to build a barrier between us.

I promise to always admit when I've been wrong.

I shall keep every promise whether expressed
or implied that I've made to you.

I promise to never take any other
person's side against you.

You are my darling. You are my love.

I promise to cherish and protect the trust
you've placed in me.

Thank you for allowing me to become your
husband/wife and best friend forever.

I love you_____(Name)